PRAISE FOR *BUR*

"With lucid, accessible prose and Sharon Strong recounts the seminal passages of her seven decades, tracing the fiery thread of her journey to self-knowledge, inner peace, and love. In these times when so many mature women seek continued growth and the fullest possible expression of their lives, her voice is a model of fearless honesty that concludes: Yes, we can walk through pain, through change, through loss and things we can't control. For without these experiences, there would be no art to living at all."

—LAURA PAULL, journalist, formerly of *Jewish News of Northern California* and *Huffington Post*

"This book is an inspiring roadmap into how to live a fierce life at any age—a life that embraces it all—love/loss, joy/suffering, life/death. Living fully in the last decades of life takes curiosity, courage, stamina and resilience. The rewards are a life lived without regrets and the hard earned wisdom of the crone. Read this book and be inspired!"

—PAT FERRERO, documentary filmmaker, professor of cinema at San Francisco State University

"Sharon's vignettes bring us through the depths and triumphs that have created a compassionate and fulfilling life. She lifts the veil and gives us a valuable glimpse into artistic inspiration as a journey of personal healing. I am inspired by her choice to follow her heart and seize the moment. In her words, 'Let's do it. Choose life!'"

—SEANNE SWANN, somatic practitioner

Burning Woman

Memoirs of
an Elder

Sharon Strong

SHE WRITES PRESS

Published 2022
Printed in the United States of America
Print ISBN: 978-1-64742-377-3
E-ISBN: 978-1-64742-378-0
Library of Congress Control Number: 2021924893

For information, address:
She Writes Press
1569 Solano Ave #546
Berkeley, CA 94707

Interior design by Tabitha Lahr

She Writes Press is a division of SparkPoint Studio, LLC.

For Tom,
The love of my life
And heart of my story

Masks and Other Works

Part One

Chapter 1

IT WAS LATE AFTERNOON WHEN I fell. One minute I was barreling through the living room in stockinged feet looking for my hiking boots, and the next minute, I was writhing on the floor in pain. My whole left side felt as if it had been body-slammed. My husband, Tom, came running from the back of the house when he heard me cry out and knelt beside me.

"What happened? Oh, sweetheart, are you OK?"

"I can't get up! Something's wrong. I think it's my left leg."

"Can you move at all? How's the right leg?" I lifted it, bent at the knee, then straightened it and gingerly swung it back and forth.

"Try your toes."

I flapped both feet up and down and wiggled my toes, relieved to know that I hadn't injured my spinal cord. Tom said encouragingly, "That's good. You're going to be all right. See if you can get up now."

I used my right leg for balance, hands braced against the floor, and attempted to roll onto my left knee to get into a standing position. Pain shot up from my knee to my hip, like a scream no one could hear but me. I felt cold and shaky and didn't try to move again.

"We need to go to the ER. There's no way I can get into the car. Will you call 911?"

Tom made the call, then laid down behind me, curling his long body around mine, the way we spooned together in bed. I could feel his warm breath against my neck. He whispered over and over, "It's going to be OK. I love you, sweetheart. It's going to be OK," the way one comforts a child. But I couldn't get up, and it was not OK.

It took forever for the ambulance to come. Like a wounded animal, my mind focused on survival. *Be still. Don't cry. They're on their way.* Tom asked, "How long do you think it's going to take?"

"I don't know." The pain was becoming more intense.

There was a sharp knock on the front door. Tom rose to open it. Four paramedics, three men and a woman, spilled into the narrow space where I lay on my left side, between the couch and the door. I heard their voices above me, the thump and scrape of their boots on the cement floor. A rush of cold air. Flashing red lights outside in the darkness told me it was nighttime.

The atmosphere vibrated with a sense of urgency. Leaning over my body, they fired off questions: "What happened? When did it happen? What's your level of pain? Can you walk?"

Tom answered for me, "She fell an hour ago. No. She can't walk."

Someone said, "We've got to carry her." I groaned as they shifted my body onto a gurney. Two EMTs at my head and two at my feet lifted me up and took me out to the waiting ambulance. Every movement was unbearable. I wanted to scream out in pain, but a voice inside said, *Don't cry. Be still.* They shoved me as gently as they could into the back, strapped me in, and shut the double doors. I could feel every pothole as they drove slowly down our gravel road, aware that when the driver turned left onto the paved road, it would take us to the hospital an hour away. My husband followed in his car. I heard someone moaning. It was me.

I DON'T KNOW HOW TOM GOT TO the hospital before we did, but he was there when we arrived at the emergency entrance. I was wheeled past other patients lying on gurneys in the hallway and whisked into a patient room. A friendly male nurse took my vitals and said, "I'll be right back with the doc, and we'll get you something for pain. You're scheduled for X-rays, but there's a couple people ahead of you. This Memorial Day weekend is nuts."

When Tom and I were alone, I cried for the first time since the fall. He held me gently, murmuring, "It's OK, I'm here." I clung to him like a scared little girl, wanting him to make it all go away.

While we waited for X-rays, I was given one pain medication after another with names like bad guys in a 1950s film noir: Fentanyl, Dilaudid, morphine. I'm a lightweight when it comes to drugs. Within seconds of each injection, my heart started racing, my face was on fire, and I was nauseous.

They gave me something to vomit into, and suddenly I'm ten years old, on my knees, elbows on the toilet seat, holding my head in my hands. It's the middle of the night, and I'm sick. My stomach begins heaving, and I throw up. The vomit smells bad and tastes nasty. When it stops, I wash my mouth out and get back into bed. I don't call for my mother. I know not to make noise if my parents are in their bedroom with the door closed. I'd learned early on to take care of myself.

Tom looked worried as he watched the ER nurse wheel my gurney down the hall for X-rays. He wasn't allowed to go with me. The nurse transferred me to a cold metal table and

left. It was just me and the X-ray technician, a man of indeter-
minate age in blue scrubs with no expression on his face. He
made no eye contact, just told me, "Lie still," in a perfunctory
tone. I closed my eyes, listening to the low hum of the X-ray
machine, until it was over. When the technician said, "Turn
over," I thought, *Oh my God. I can't do that*, and I told him
so. Unmoved by the desperation in my eyes, he positioned a
foam back support and rolled my body over on my side as I
groaned. It felt as if I was going to pass out as the machine
took the last image.

I have no memory of my return trip to the ER. The on-call
doctor came back in, asked how I was doing, and gave a cursory
look at my chart. Pointing to the ghostly images of my left hip
and thigh bone on a small X-ray screen hanging on the wall,
he said, "Hip looks good, but you have a fractured femur.
You'll need surgery. Can't do it tonight. We're pretty jammed
because of the holiday. Should be sometime tomorrow. Your
surgeon is scheduled to see you in the morning, and he'll
explain everything."

It was after midnight when I was transferred to the orthopedic surgical unit and Tom went home. I was given morphine
intravenously to help me sleep, but it seemed that I lay awake
most of the night listening to the hospital sounds, like bees at
work in a medical-industrial hive.

Tom arrived in the midmorning, looking more tired than I
did. There was nothing we could do but wait for the surgeon
to come in and tell us when surgery would be scheduled and
when the pain would stop. I felt like an addict waiting for a fix.
The doctor arrived at three in the afternoon, apologizing for
the holiday delay. He explained that because my hip socket was
healthy, he'd only be doing a partial hip replacement, recon-
structing the broken femur. I went into surgery at eight o'clock
that night.

Coming out of the anesthesia felt to me what it must be like for a newborn to leave the womb. I was completely dependent on others for help. I peered around the recovery room, unsure of where I was. Tom was there, his voice soothing, "I love you, sweetheart. I'm here. The surgery went well." I was in no pain. Bless anesthesia. Tom kissed me good night and drove home as I drifted off into a dreamless sleep.

DAY TWO IN THE HOSPITAL WAS ENTIRELY different. Before I had finished breakfast, two women came into my room with a shiny new aluminum walker. The taller one said with practiced cheerfulness, "I'm Sandra, your physical therapist, and this is my assistant, Mallory. We're going to take you for a walk." I hadn't even gotten out of bed yet to pee on my own. I must have looked incredulous, because she began to reassure me that most patients walk the day of surgery. The PT was wearing cool-looking workout pants and Nike sneakers. Her assistant was in scrubs. I had on a standard-issue gown that tied in the back, socks with rubber tread, and nothing else. I wondered fleetingly if this was appropriate dress, then thought, *What the hell. Let's go.*

Mallory stood next to me to provide support while Sandra instructed me to sit up carefully, pivot my body and both legs in one fluid motion to the side of the bed, and place my feet firmly on the floor. I did as I was told. I felt overcome by dizziness, and my bravado evaporated. Sandra said, "Good," smiling at me as if I were a well-behaved toddler. "You're doing so good."

I took a few deep breaths and said, "OK. What's next?"

"Now it's time to stand." She positioned the walker in front of me. "Take hold of the handles and find your balance. When you're ready, use the strength of your arms to stand up."

My body felt as if it weighed two hundred pounds. I stood up using my right leg, barely resting the left one on the floor. I was sweating, afraid to put any pressure on the wounded leg. With the physical therapist on one side of me and her assistant on the other, I hobbled out of my room and turned left. She said, "Let's see if we can go to the end of the corridor." With each step, the tension in my body and in my head began to relax. My left leg hurt, but it was manageable. I completed one round of the corridor that wrapped around the orthopedic unit and felt as if I had run a marathon. Walking was freedom. Walking meant that I could go home.

Walking was an iconic event in my childhood. I walked at eight months, when most babies are just beginning to master crawling. My dad was in pilot's training in the Army Air Force during World War II, and I was the first baby in my parents' circle of friends. When he and his buddies came home on leave, part of their entertainment was training me to walk. I was a willing recruit. At seven months, I could walk a couple of steps, as I held onto one end of a string that my dad was holding. A few weeks later, he dropped the string, and I just kept on going.

This is a developmental milestone for any kid, the beginning of independence. Let go of the string and keep on walking became my primary survival strategy. In some ways, it still is. Getting attention for accomplishment was love I could earn, but it meant doing what my dad wanted me to do to please him. Was I ready to walk on my own at eight months? Probably not. Did I discover in my baby way how to stand and take the first steps because of my own curiosity? I don't think so. What I couldn't have known then was how fragile my connection to my father was, how prophetic it was that he let go first.

"I walked!" I announced to Tom when he came that afternoon. "I walked by myself all the way around the unit! I can go home tomorrow!" It felt like a milestone of a different sort, tinged with irony. I was seventy-three years old and I could walk—unassisted—using a walker. An unnamed fear clutched at my joy. I was on an uncharted journey that I didn't want and didn't choose, and I didn't know where I was going.

Chapter 2

I HAD ONLY BEEN HOME TWO DAYS and had cabin fever. I felt imprisoned in my body, and the one bar of my prison was a metal rod embedded in my femur. It ached. It kept me awake at night. I had to get out.

Because I couldn't bend over, my husband strapped sensible hiking sandals on my feet. I hobbled out the front door and down a brick walkway, clinging to my walker. It felt like a cage I could take with me. When I reached the dirt driveway, the wheels wouldn't roll over the ruts and stones, so I alternately pushed and carried it. I was determined and scared. *What if I fall? Breathe, one step, two steps, don't take your eyes off the trail. Breathe, step, breathe, step.* My feet and eyes registered every variation in the topography. At some point, I realized that I knew how to do this. But how? A memory surfaced, my first trek in the Nepal Himalayas, six years earlier, at age sixty-seven, learning how to walk at high elevation on rough terrain, leaning on my trekking poles.

The journey began at 9,000 feet, on a dirt road a short distance out of the small village of Lukla, following my woman guide. As we climbed, the trail narrowed, skimming the edge of a precipice that dropped straight down to a raging river.

Up ahead, I saw a delicate suspension bridge festooned with prayer flags. It was obvious we needed to cross that bridge. *Step, breathe, step, breathe. Never take your eyes off the trail.* Yes. I knew how to do this.

Our driveway was about the length of a football field. I went up and back three times. My first "trek" after surgery was a success.

Chapter 3

THE FIRST TIME I VENTURED BEYOND our property, I drove my car with Tom as passenger to the follow-up appointment with my surgeon. Driving was another milestone. Hyperaware of my left leg and the long incision that ran diagonally across my left cheek, I tentatively got into the driver's seat butt-first and carefully swung both legs into position. Sitting behind the wheel felt strange, as if my center of balance was off. With some trepidation, I turned the key in the ignition, stepped on the accelerator, and headed for Angels Camp.

I typically drove the road into town at sixty miles per hour, only slowing down when I could spy the sheriff, who often lay in wait just off the highway. On this day, driving forty-five miles per hour seemed too fast. I felt tentative, like a teenager taking her first driving test, or an old lady who was afraid of getting busted and losing her driver's license.

When we arrived, I gingerly got out of the car and walked into the waiting room leaning on a cane. Two women were already there, two old women. One leaned heavily on a walker. The other sat stooped over, her back bent like the curve of my cane. They could have been my age. I looked away, judging them and myself. I felt ashamed, terrified to call them my peers.

In the exam room, I was given ugly blue paper shorts big enough to fit my husband. This was certainly different from the ugly paper dressing gown I was familiar with. A nurse came in and led me down the hall for an X-ray. Bereft of my jeans, clad in a long-sleeved T-shirt and shorts that I had to hold up with my left hand while balancing on the cane with my right, I looked like shit and knew it. In defiance, I walked like a model strutting down the runway, with no one watching but me.

Back in the room, perched on a hard exam table waiting for the surgeon, I picked up the only two magazines available, *Concealed Carry: The Ultimate Resource for Responsibly Armed Americans*, and *Vogue*. Fascinated and horrified by the weird juxtaposition, I looked at the gun magazine. It was filled with images of lethal weapons. Never before had I seen a magazine about handguns in a doctor's office. My last opportunity for distraction was the women's fashion magazine. Flipping through the pages, I saw a model, barely out of her teens, in stiletto heels and wearing a tight, pin-striped wool skirt and tailored jacket, revealing perfect cleavage from neck to waist. I felt sad. I did not belong in either world, nor did I want to.

My surgeon came in to admire his handiwork. The X-rays confirmed that he had done an excellent job. The healthy bone of my left femur was healing around a titanium spike. The cobalt steel ball on top of it fit perfectly into my hip socket. It felt somehow cool to have a bionic leg. No follow-up appointments were necessary. The surgeon gave me a referral for physical therapy and released me to return to work the next day.

Chapter 4

THREE WEEKS AND ONE DAY AFTER surgery, I returned to work. I'm a psychologist and have been in private practice in San Andreas, the county seat, for almost twenty years. The discovery of gold in California in 1849 and Mark Twain's short story "The Celebrated Jumping Frog of Calaveras County" are its two claims to fame.

My commute to work takes about thirty minutes, following the winding curves of Pool Station Road through a rural landscape of vineyards, grazing cattle, twenty-acre ranchettes, and an abandoned cement plant. It's like a driving meditation, but this morning I felt apprehensive. The walker and cane were in the back seat of my car. I had already swapped the bentwood rocker I usually sat in for a sturdy, straight-backed chair, and I had a bottle of extra-strength ibuprofen in my purse. My schedule was full, and my clients were happy I was back. What was going on?

I tried something I often did to clear my mind to make space for what my clients would be bringing in. It was a dialogue, and it went something like this:

Just relax and feel into your body. (And for God's sake, don't close your eyes!)

What are you feeling?
Scared—and sad.
Where are you feeling it? How does it feel?
Tight in my gut, and my heart feels heavy.
What are you afraid of?
I don't know. Well, I do know the obvious. This is my first day with my clients. I'm not 100 percent. I'm not sure how this is going to work, getting up and down, hobbling around with the walker, using the stairs. And I'm tired.

I began to feel strangely alone and incredibly sad when thoughts about my father began to intrude, one painful memory after another. *This isn't a good time.*

Yeah, it is.

My little brother and I are in the back seat of my uncle's car. He's been babysitting us during the day while our mom is at work. Our dad is supposed to be taking care of us, but he's taken off and hasn't come home yet. Uncle Skeetz works the night shift and has to get to his job, so he's piled us into his car and says we are going to look for our dad. We drive around for a while, then park the car on a side street. He tells us we'll be OK, to just stay put. After locking the doors, he takes off into the night and is gone a long time. We're just little kids. I am six and my brother is two. The dark all around us seems huge, and we're alone. We get scared and cry a lot.

That's all I remembered. It seemed like we were always looking for my father, and he was never there.

The mind puts memories together without regard for chronology. The next one was forty-seven years later: My father is seventy-three years old. It's late at night when the phone next to my bed rings. Half asleep, I answer, "Hello." The worried voice on the line is my father's girlfriend, Anita. "Your dad's missing."

"What?"

"He drove his car to the store to get a bottle of vodka. The liquor store is just a few blocks away, and he hasn't come back. I called the police. They don't know anything. There's been no accident report."

My psychologist mind comes online. "Has this happened before?"

"Yeah. He's been having trouble remembering stuff for a while."

"For how long?"

"I don't know. Maybe six months."

"Why didn't you tell me until now?"

"He just had his annual physical. His doctor said he was in good shape for a man in his seventies."

I remember the random calls from my dad in the evening. I've been getting them for years. He repeats himself and doesn't respond to anything I say. I've assumed it's because he is drunk. I'm worried. He lives in San Diego, and I live in Berkeley. There isn't much I can do but try to go back to sleep. I have a full schedule of clients to see the next day. "Call me when you hear anything."

The next morning Anita calls back. "Your dad's OK."

He had driven the familiar route to the liquor store and gotten confused. Trying to find his way home, he turned onto a freeway on-ramp that took him out of town. Luckily, he knew enough to park the car on a residential street. Someone found him the next morning, asleep behind the wheel, and called the police. I learn that this incident was only one of many. He can present well when the situation calls for it, like seeing his primary care doctor, but it's becoming evident that he has the beginning symptoms of dementia.

The last call I get from his girlfriend is to tell me she's done, to come and get him because she isn't "going to put up with him anymore." I book a round-trip ticket to San Diego for myself and a one-way ticket for my dad for the following weekend.

By the time I got to my office, this part of the story ended. I felt like I had been in a time warp and had to shake my head to bring myself forward to Tuesday morning, 8:45. I'd see my first client in fifteen minutes. This was not new information. I had been working for years in therapy with my "family-of-origin issues." It helped to know what was going on, that the anxiety I felt wasn't just about returning to work. I got out of my car carefully and hobbled across the parking area supported by the walker, with my cane hooked over one handle. This day was important to me, to be with my clients and to do good work. But it was also clear that I had my own work to do.

Chapter 5

I GREW UP IN SOUTHERN CALIFORNIA, in one of those small, outlying cities with a forgettable name that spread out beyond the periphery of Los Angeles. My mother, father, younger brother, and I lived on Compton Boulevard, in a two-bedroom stucco bungalow, built before World War II. Across the street was a ragged field of mustard flowers and a burgeoning population of horned toads, tiny dinosaurs with spikes on their backs and smooth, dry underbellies that felt warm in my hand. We called them "horny toads." I'd bring home bouquets of pale yellow, pink, and blue wildflowers for my mom and, once in a while, a horny toad I'd try to domesticate.

One of the black-and-white photos in our family album features my father's car, a brand-new silver Jaguar Mark VII sedan, proudly parked on the front lawn. It's strange that I can remember the make of his car. I learned later that it cost more than our house.

My dad was six feet tall, tanned, with dark wavy hair. Even as a kid, I knew that women thought he was handsome. A natural athlete, he had been a star quarterback in high school. In his hometown, he was still a legend. He drove fast cars, wore expensive shoes, and bought his clothes at an exclusive men's shop. The rest of us lived as if we were still in the Depression that both my parents grew up in. I never understood why it was OK for my father to have so much more than his wife and children. My mother never talked about it, and I never asked. There was so much we didn't talk about.

My mother's father left his family for another woman when his three daughters were children. Times were hard for everybody at the end of the Great Depression, but especially for a divorced woman on her own with teenage girls to raise. My mother, the middle child, rarely told stories about her childhood, but I remember one. She and her sisters were each given a pair of white oxfords in the spring, worn with the ankle socks that were in style in the 1940s. When fall came, the girls would dye them black, so they could be worn through the winter until the next spring, when they would get a new pair of white shoes.

My mother always worked and went to college: bachelor's degree, teaching credential, master's in education, and eventually a PhD. She taught me that women get things done. Women get degrees and become professionals. She was a feminist before the women's liberation movement began, but at home, my father was king. He got whatever he wanted. He lived however he wanted. When I was growing up, this was what I knew of family, my brother and me and our mom living in a separate world from "Daddy," our father in name only.

Chapter 6

THE MAN WHO WAS NEVER THERE FOR ME suddenly needed me to take care of him. He'd squandered his life just as I was carving out the freedom, in middle age, to live my own. I didn't want this, but I couldn't turn my back on him.

Anita and my dad had a long history. Their affair ended his marriage to the woman he had an affair with while he was married to my mother. They had run a small business together. They both loved cats. They drank together. I thought he and Anita had reached a kind of quid pro quo in their relationship. But it became crystal clear that her decision to leave him was final when she told me about his erratic behavior, increasingly severe memory loss, angry outbursts, and sexual obsession. Forgetting his way home and being lost for twenty-four hours was only the tip of the iceberg.

He could be engaging when the attention was on him, for example during his annual checkup. Based on what my father selectively reported to the doctor, he diagnosed normal aging in a physically fit seventy-three-year-old man. When I consulted with him over the phone about my plan for my dad to live near me in a board and care home, the doctor said that was appropriate. He thought my father would do well in a home-care environment. However, he hadn't lived with my father, and neither had I.

It was 1997. I was fifty-three, married to a writer, and living upstairs in an old, tenants-in-common house in Berkeley. To get to our place, a two-bedroom, one-bath flat, one ascended a wooden staircase that spiraled around a corner of the house. Our downstairs neighbor was a National Public Radio announcer from the 1960s whose companion was an aging pit bull. A French-Canadian woman and her young daughter lived in the mother-in-law cottage in back.

Berkeley was mecca, the place I had longed to be in the 1970s. So what if I was twenty years late? This was my time. Whole Foods was a short walk to the corner of Ashby and Telegraph. I could bicycle to UC Berkeley and see foreign films anytime I wanted at two different theaters downtown. I marched through the streets of San Francisco protesting the war in the Gulf and stood in silent vigil outside the gates of San Quentin State Prison, opposing the death penalty. I rode BART to the city to take painting classes at the Academy of Art University. I had come here to escape the oppressive conservatism of Orange County, where I had lived from the age of ten, to create a life far from the scene of my childhood. There was no way my dad fit into this picture. But Anita wanted him out, and I had less than a week to find a board and care facility near my home that he could afford on Social Security.

My father had two adult children. I ask myself now why I took sole responsibility in the beginning. I was the elder, a mental health professional living in an urban area with an abundance of resources for "senior citizens." My younger brother lived three hours away, in one of the poorest rural counties in California. He also had a chip on his shoulder. After our parents' divorce, my mother wanted her freedom, so she sent my thirteen-year-old brother to live with our father and his former mistress, who had become his second wife. They were two people who knew nothing about raising an angry teenager. Thirty-six years later, he still carried resentment and wanted to be only peripherally involved.

That's the most obvious explanation for why I stepped up. However, under the surface—way under the surface—was a little girl still waiting for her daddy to come home. Maybe now he would.

All of this felt surreal. In one week, I would fly to San Diego, pick up my dad and all of his belongings, and fly home with him. But my home would not be his home. He was going to be living with strangers for the first time in his life since he served in the military.

Chapter 7

ON OUR FLIGHT FROM SAN DIEGO to San Francisco, my father sat next to me in the rear of the airplane. His carry-on bag was stowed overhead, with all the clothes he owned. A cardboard box rested on his lap. He encircled it with his arms as if it contained treasure. I had no idea what was inside. He was nervous in the way that meant he needed a drink, toughing it out, trying hard to be strong. I could feel his vulnerability and wanted to put my arms around him and tell him it was going to be OK. But I knew it wasn't, and so did he.

About thirty minutes into the flight, he turned to me and said in a voice so subdued I could barely hear him, "Sharon, you're a doctor. You help people whose minds don't work. Maybe you could fix mine." My breath caught in my throat. He knew. There was no way to mask his despair. I told him that he was going to live near me, in a nice neighborhood, with people he would be comfortable with.

I had lived in Berkeley for eight years, and he had never visited me. How could I describe my town, and what was coming for him, in a way he could understand? I didn't even know what was coming. It was as if we were suspended in space and time, but soon we would land, and the clock would start ticking again.

My dad sat quietly beside me as we drove from SFO on Route 101, cruising the outskirts of San Francisco. The Transamerica Building looked like a futuristic castle at the center of a magical city. He said little as we crossed the Bay Bridge and followed I-580 east, dropping down into Berkeley. Occasionally, I looked sideways at him. He was staring out the window, as if he had landed on another planet. I don't remember what I said to him. There were no words that would make this different or better. We were both going into the unknown, but there was a huge difference. After I dropped him off with strangers, I would be going home.

We pulled up to the curb in front of my dad's board and care home. I got out and grabbed his suitcase from the back seat. He carried his box. Had it been on his lap the whole time? We followed cement paving stones up to the front door and rang the bell. In a dark corner of my mind, it felt like the iconic scene from the film *Dead Man Walking.* I put a smile on my face to greet the middle-aged couple who ran the board and care. I introduced my dad, and they smiled at him. We were all smiling perfunctorily, except for Dad, whose expression was unreadable. They showed us through the house, a 1940s bungalow not unlike the one I grew up in, except that there were sunny yellow walls in the kitchen, more than the usual number of recliners in the living room, and chintz everywhere—curtains, dining room chairs, the couch. The door to my father's bedroom was open, and we walked in as if we were weekend guests. The couple closed the door behind us so we could "get settled." Dad sat down heavily on the twin bed. I didn't want to leave him all alone, but I didn't know what to say. It felt as if I was doing something wrong, leaving him there. I unpacked his clothes. They fit in one drawer of the dresser. I put his box on the bedside table where he could see it. Dinner would be served in a half hour, so I said, "Goodbye, Daddy. I love you. I'll come back tomorrow."

Chapter 8

I WISH TELLING THIS PART OF our story was easier. It's not. I want to write with respect and compassion for my father's and my experience, and the experiences of other families caring for aging husbands and wives, fathers and mothers, who pass away in mind and soul long before their bodies die. Watching the one you love deteriorate until you can no longer recognize him or her, and caring for them after they have lost the capacity to know who you are, is unspeakably painful. My professional understanding became personal. I came to know that Alzheimer's affects the whole family. For some patients, this prolonged end of life can be relatively peaceful, especially for those with close family ties and financial support. It is very different for people lacking those resources, and especially difficult when darker aspects of the individual's personality surface to be faced by caregivers and when the Alzheimer's patient can no longer be held responsible for behavior in the present or in the past.

I picked up my father after breakfast the next morning. It was time for him to check out Berkeley, to see where I lived, and for us to have lunch together. It was strange showing him around the place I had lived in for almost a decade and introducing him to my husband for the first time. I never imagined this would happen—Dad coming for a visit—and had long ago let go of any expectation that he would be a meaningful part of my life. I also knew that we could not have done this the night before. It would have been too confusing. He had to learn that his home was the board and care and meet the people who would be his housemates, three dependent adults around his age, and the couple who ran the facility. After lunch at a Thai restaurant near the BART station, I took him home. His first day went OK.

In retrospect, I realize that he didn't have a chance. His futile efforts to adapt broke my heart. I was angry with the doctor in San Diego. I was angry with myself. How could I have been so naive? He had no car. He had no Anita. He had no alcohol. He wanted to find his lost life, so he went looking for it. He walked. Every day he walked, farther and farther from the board and care. At first, he talked to me proudly about all the street names he was learning, all the neighborhoods he discovered. *This is good*, I thought.

I bought him an ID bracelet with his name and my name, phone number, and address in case he got lost. The first time it happened, two friendly cops brought him to my front door and turned him over to me, saying, "You'd better keep an eye on him." I took him back to the board and care. The folks said they'd keep a closer eye on him, but they could not. He was becoming more agitated, restless, and more confused. I hoped the board and care home would become familiar, but his mind was already moving back in time. He began asking when Anita would come and get him. He wanted to know where his old Mercedes was parked. He wanted a drink. My logical answers to his frantic questions made no sense to him. By the end of the first month, he was becoming angry and more reactive. I started to feel strung out, trying to work full-time and take care of him. Would I get another one of those late-night calls saying he had disappeared?

My dad was picked up a couple more times, wandering the streets of his neighborhood, not knowing where his home was. It had been only six weeks since I had first dropped him off at the board and care. His last escape was in the middle of the night. When I got the call, I wasn't surprised. He had been apprehended climbing over fences and into people's backyards, trying to get away. He was taken into custody and hospitalized at Alta Bates on a "5150," a seventy-two-hour involuntary hold, because he was a danger to himself and a perceived danger to others. The psychiatrist on staff diagnosed him with Alzheimer's disease.

The doctor in San Diego had assured me before I brought him to Berkeley that my father would do well in a board and care. The Alzheimer's diagnosis shattered any belief I had that this minimally restrictive living situation would work. I wanted a way out of this mess, for my dad and for me, but there was no way out. I had taken on way too much responsibility for him, and I had little control. He needed to be in a more secure facility. I knew that disrupting the familiar environment of a person with the beginning symptoms of dementia could exacerbate them, but Anita had kicked him out. I was angry with her too. What choice did I have but to find somewhere else for him to live? I felt cornered, and my dad was in the corner with me, out of his mind. If I were the therapist sitting across from me, I'd know what to say, but I had never done this before with a family member, and I didn't know what to do next. His life and mine had become enmeshed, twenty-four seven. This was not a fifty-minute session, and my professional training could not protect me from the unrelenting responsibility and heartbreak of trying to take care of my father as he was deteriorating so rapidly. Even though we were running out of options, I had no choice but to keep trying, and neither did he.

The nice couple at the board and care said they could not take him back. They would lose their license if he ran away again. The "5150" became a "5250" because he was still a danger, and he could legally be held for two more weeks. At the end of that time, treatment and medication had helped manage his symptoms. A social worker at the hospital found an Alzheimer's facility in San Francisco that would take him. His application for Social Security disability benefits had not yet been approved, so my mother loaned him the $3,000 he needed to be admitted. She told me that she had never stopped loving him.

His new digs were on the third floor of a locked Alzheimer's unit in the middle of San Francisco, on a busy thoroughfare that runs from the Mission to the Marina District. The only way to get in and out was by way of an elevator directly across the corridor from the front desk. He couldn't escape.

At first, he seemed to be settling in. In his mind, he had regressed to his thirties. With restraint peeling away like the skin of an onion, he began to live his secret life out in the open. At this point, I didn't know if he knew who I was, but he always enjoyed my visits.

One in particular stands out: I'm standing in front of the elevator doors. They open like curtains going up on a theater performance. My dad is right there at center stage, smiling his half-seductive, half-serious smile. He greets me with a hug and shows me around the dry-cleaning business he owned while I was growing up. The nursing staff, mostly Filipino women, look diminutive bustling around my tall father. My dad says proudly, "Look at those girls! Look how hard they're working." He means the "girls" who had worked for him. He's so convincing that I can almost see them wheeling huge canvas bags filled with garments to the machines and smell the chemical that always lingered in clothes he dry-cleaned for us. He takes special pride in introducing me to his girlfriend, also a patient. Of course, there would always be another girlfriend.

When I'm ready to leave, I check in with the nursing staff to ask how he's doing. They tell me his nickname is "Lover

Boy." As I walk back to the recreation room to say goodbye, I see him sitting close to his girlfriend, a small, plump, white-haired woman. They're holding hands and watching television. Not wanting to disturb them, I turn away with a wry smile on my face and descend in the elevator three floors to street level, grateful that he's safe and seems happy.

Driving home, I ponder my dad's experience of Alzheimer's. He's no longer afraid, no longer confused, no longer alone. His dementia has erased forty years of memories. Existential questions about the meaning of life for people with Alzheimer's spin in my mind. I have no answers. It's enough that my dad seems to be at peace. He's doing so well after the first few weeks that he gets a one-day pass to come to my house for Thanksgiving. The peace would be short-lived.

AT THE END OF JANUARY, I GOT A CALL informing me that Dad had punched a male patient and injured him, but not badly. My father had been a boxer in his youth. At six feet tall and 180 pounds, he still had the strength of a man half his age. The man he hurt also had dementia and could not protect himself. There was no way he could have understood why he had been attacked. My father was becoming more agitated and quick to anger. The girlfriend no longer sat next to him holding his hand when I visited. For the time being, the staff seemed to be managing him, and at least he couldn't escape. Until he did, riding the elevator down to the ground floor. He snuck out at the end of visiting hours. This time no one called me in the middle of the night. The head nurse waited until the next morning to tell me that the San Francisco Police Department had an all-points bulletin out for him, and the staff would keep me updated.

Oh, Dad. Now what? I was scared for him, imagining him running the streets of San Francisco. I was scared for anyone unwittingly running into him. This wasn't Berkeley. The city was huge, fast, and some of the neighborhoods were dangerous. Even as I waited and worried, part of me wanted him to run free, to escape the city, to escape the prison of his deteriorating brain, and, in the words of Dylan Thomas, to "not go gentle into that good night. Rage, rage against the dying of the light."

He was found within twenty-four hours and placed in the geriatric unit at San Francisco General Hospital. When I visited him, I found him strapped into a metal chair with a tray attached so that it looked like an adult high chair. He was so sedated he couldn't eat the lunch that was right in front of him. He couldn't coordinate picking up the hamburger and bringing it to his mouth. I could tell he was hungry, so I began to feed him. First, I tried to cut bites of the hamburger and bun, spearing them on the end of a fork. It didn't work, so I pulled off pieces and fed him with my fingers. I felt like a mother feeding her baby bird. I could feel his lips when I put the food in his mouth. He was so vulnerable and helpless. Feeding my daddy, I felt vulnerable and helpless. Silent tears streamed down my face. He finished his hamburger, and I gave him a drink through a straw.

Needing some space, I walked down a long corridor, following the haunting sound of classical music, and found an open door into a large room occupied by an old man and an old woman. The old man was hunched over the keyboard of an upright piano playing a Bach concerto as if there was no one in the room but him and the music, and then I realized that the woman standing close to him must be his wife.

She smiled at me and said quietly, "It's the only time he comes to life. Music is the only thing he remembers." I listened for a time with my eyes closed, then turned and walked back to where my father had fallen asleep in his chair. I kissed him tenderly on his forehead so I wouldn't wake him, and I stopped at the nurse's station to tell her of my concern about his level of sedation. She said she would talk with the psychiatrist. I didn't know what would happen next. We were running out of options.

It took a couple of weeks to find appropriate placement for my father, a large, single-story, locked Alzheimer's facility in a small town in Central California. It was completely enclosed in a ten-foot-high chain-link fence from which he couldn't escape. I was able to visit occasionally. He was medicated and well cared for, and he seemed content. My brother lived close enough to see him weekly and was willing to take over as the contact person. When he no longer knew who I was, I stopped going. He died two years later.

Chapter 9

I CREATED MY FIRST MASK AT THE beginning of my father's descent into hell. Art has always been my passion. The years of completing a PhD and getting licensed as a psychologist were barely behind me when I moved to Berkeley and started a private practice. I began taking painting classes at the Academy of Art in San Francisco to get back into the creative groove and to meet other artists. When I moved my father to Berkeley, I was working on an autobiographical trilogy of figurative paintings. The third painting, life-size, was inspired by a nightmare I'd had when he was in San Francisco General Hospital; it was of a woman dancing alone, her face a mask of anger. When it was done, I was disappointed. I hadn't taken enough risks.

The gesture of the figure worked, but the mask looked flat. I needed to do the painting again, starting by making an actual mask of rage and letting it guide me. Searching through some VHS tapes on handicrafts in the basement of the old Berkeley Public Library, I found one on mask-making, took it home, and played it through twice, taking careful notes. With a sense of anticipation, I took my list of materials to Amsterdam Art on University Avenue. It was my favorite art store, because all of the clerks were artists. I found a guy dressed in jeans and a tie-dyed T-shirt and asked him where the plaster gauze, papier-mâché, and wooden sculptor's tools were. He was curious about what I was going to do with them, so I began to explain about the painting, the dream, and the mask. I felt embarrassed and taken by surprise when my eyes teared up. What was I getting into? He looked at me sympathetically, not saying much, and took my stuff to the register as I chose tubes of acrylic paint in intense reds, yellows, blues, black, metallic copper, and gold. This was the beginning of a creative and a spiritual journey that would change my life.

It began with making a plaster gauze form of my face in the bathroom, looking into a mirror above the sink. I wrapped my hair in a length of Handi-Wrap, tied in back like a plastic kerchief, and slathered my face with Vaseline. I dipped strips of plaster-saturated fabric into a bowl of warm water and smoothed them over my skin. My familiar face disappeared, until nothing recognizable was left but intense green eyes looking back at me out of a ghostly white mask. When the plaster set, I took it off and laid it on the worktable in my studio. Removing the mask felt like hatching out of a fragile eggshell.

When the life mask was completely dry, I used it as a base and sculpted a separate mask over it. With trembling fingers, in the solitude of my studio, I shaped wet papier-mâché into my first art mask. A contorted, angry face began to come to life. What was happening? All I knew was that fear was driving my work. Fear and exhilaration. There was no sound but the rhythmic pounding of my heart, as sculpted hair seemed to burst into flames at the touch of my hands. Into a grimacing mouth with jagged teeth of broken glass, I slid a stiletto tongue. Could I tell this much truth? The mask had its own, uncompromising, visual language. This was not artistic abstraction. This was me—my rage unmasked. I stood in the middle of my studio and screamed and sobbed at the futility of it all. I could not hold on to my father. No matter what I did, he continued to slip through my fingers. I was still clinging to the fucking string, and there was no one there.

I created my first mask thinking it would be an art object. I did not know that mask-making was a ritual as old as human-kind. I did not know that, for me, it would be impossible to make a mask without participating in the ritual. I did not know that my heart was starving for intimate contact with my own soul.

The spirit of the mask prepared me for what was to come. It became my guide through the nightmare of letting go of the father I never had. When he was dying, I went to see him one last time. He looked so frail beneath the white blanket, the skin on his face almost transparent. His body was still, and he did not respond to my touch. I stroked my father's face and placed my hand gently on his chest, feeling it rising and falling. I whispered, "I love you, Daddy. You can go now. It's OK. You can go."

The second mask was born with its mouth open in sound-less grief, inside another face with a mouth open in soundless grief, like nested Russian dolls. With loving hands, I created my father's death mask. The shards of glass that had expressed primal rage in the first mask were transformed into a halo, or a crown of glittering thorns, depending upon how it caught the light. Was the grief his or mine? Perhaps it belonged to both of us.

After my father's death, the third mask emerged, a phoenix rising from the ashes of his life. Its wings were a collage of paper feathers, cut from military documents I found in the meager store of mementos in his cardboard box. While in training to become a pilot in World War II, he had been court-martialed for participating in an aerial stunt that almost cost his life and the life of his copilot. My father was grounded for the duration of the war, banished to a recruiting office in St. Louis, Missouri. In an intimate dialogue with these pieces of his history, I made wings for my dad out of the record of his failure. And the ashes at the base of the phoenix mask? They are his. Was this permissible? I only know that it had to be.

I never went back to do a second painting of the woman in my nightmare. The art and ritual of mask-making determined my trajectory as an artist for the next fifteen years.

A YEAR AFTER MY FATHER DIED, I FELT ready to show his masks in a public venue. I responded to a call for artists to perform at an event in Berkeley called "Works in the Works." My application was accepted. As a transpersonal psychologist, I believe that, at an unconscious level, we carry the bones of our psychic ancestors with us. When we heal wounded parts of ourselves, we heal our inner ancestors as well. My father's "bones" were literally part of the phoenix mask. Perhaps working on a performance piece would heal both of us.

A few weeks later, while doing improvisational dance with a woman who taught movement for healing, this poem surfaced, complete, in my mind:

> *I am dancing on my father's grave*
> *After scattering his ashes*
> *His flesh is cinders*
> *And his bones are shattered*
> *Flesh of my flesh*
> *Bone of my bone*
> *Now our lives are both in ashes*

I was stunned. This poem had come from the energy of the dance, with no conscious intention on my part. The synchronicity with the phoenix mask was obvious. "Dancing on my Father's Grave" became the title for my performance and the centerpiece of the work.

It also raised a question that would not go away. Although my marriage of ten years was floundering, how was the rest of my life in ashes? I was a fifty-five-year-old psychologist with a successful private practice. I was making art that was meaningful to me and to others. Friends and family were loving and supportive. My father was gone, but he had been mostly gone all of my life. I didn't get it.

I thought the healing work with my father was complete. I had begun grieving his death long before he died physically. I was at peace knowing that we had loved each other the best we knew how. But the ritual of mask-making had opened a door into a subterranean part of my mind, and I realized that my connection to him was much deeper than I had understood. Looking back, I believed that my knowledge as a psychologist was a kind of talisman that would protect me from any more emotional pain with my father. Although I lived my life on the surface as if nothing had changed, a part of me felt increasingly disconnected from a world that had once felt familiar.

AS THE MONTHS WORE ON, I BEGAN to crave solitude. I wanted nothing more than to be alone on forty acres I owned in the Sierra foothills, northeast of Sacramento. Alone in a small studio I had recently built there. Alone with the gray pine, manzanita, and toyon that grew in wild disarray on the land. Alone with the haunting question, *How is my life in ashes?*

A quote from Rainer Maria Rilke in *Letters to a Young Poet* kept nagging at my mind, something about loving the questions themselves. Before leaving for a weekend in the studio, I pulled out a worn copy from my bookshelf and shoved it into my bag as I was walked out the door. Later that night, I built a fire in the woodstove and curled up with Rilke and a glass of wine.

I found the quote easily because I had turned a corner of the page down years before, when I'd first read it:

> Have patience with everything unresolved in your heart and . . . try to love *the questions themselves* as if they were locked rooms or books written in a very foreign language. Don't search for the answers, which could not be given to you now, because you would not be able to live them. And the point is, to live everything. *Live* the questions now. Perhaps then, someday far in the future, you will gradually, without even noticing it, live your way into the answer.

Rilke was twenty-six when he wrote those words to a nineteen-year-old cadet in the Austro-Hungarian Army. His advice moved me deeply. Yes, love the questions. Yes, live the questions now. Yes, *live everything!* But I was also pissed off. I had filed for divorce. I was not twenty-something. I didn't have *time* to *gradually* live my way into the answer! I wanted the answer now.

I spent more time on the land and wanted less to go home. The studio, a rustic pole barn with a loft, became my second home in the small community of Mountain Ranch. In 2000, I moved to Calaveras County, population forty thousand, less than half the number of people living in the city of Berkeley.

Chapter 10

MY TRANSITION FROM URBAN to rural culture, from Berkeley to Calaveras County, took a year. I lost the Berkeley house in the divorce. My children were grown. It was just me, for the first time in my adult life. I moved into the kind of housing that divorced people choose when they don't know where they're going to land. My temporary home in the Bay Area was a three-room apartment, a "railroad flat," so named because the living room, bedroom, and bathroom were lined up like compartments on a train. Except that it didn't move. Everything else around it did. Located on a corner where Stanford and San Pablo Avenues cross each other, one of the busiest intersections in Oakland, California, cars and delivery trucks, buses, police cars, and ambulances were in motion twenty-four hours a day. The cacophony of screeching brakes, screaming sirens, and horns honking was unrelenting. It seemed as if there was no night at night, only the sulfuric, yellow glow of streetlights. The only peaceful place was the Siddha Yoga Ashram on the opposite corner, standing in white-stucco palatial splendor. Some of my fellow apartment dwellers were devotees of Swami Muktananda, and if my bedroom window was open, I would occasionally hear them chanting in the small garden at the back of our building.

During that year, I continued working as a psychologist at my office in the East Bay, seeing clients Tuesday through Thursday. Every other four-day "weekend," I'd drive after work on Thursday night to Mountain Ranch. It felt like a typical child-visitation arrangement between divorced parents, only I was the parent as well as the child, and "the child" in me needed to play. The creative energy awakened by working on my dad's trilogy of masks needed expression. After my father's life and my marriage ended, it was necessary for my emotional survival.

I vividly remember what it was like to drive up the dirt road to my small barn house after work. It felt as if I had been in unceasing motion for three days. I'd park near the back door and sit completely still with my hands in my lap, eyes closed, enveloped in the velvet darkness. Only when I could feel the silence would I get out of the car. Looking up into the night sky at endless stars flung across the delicate fabric of the Milky Way, I knew I was home.

I learned to love this wild country whose foothills had sheltered robbers and writers, men lusting for gold, and the women who followed them. Small towns with histories linked to the gold rush are nestled in the valleys. Only abandoned mines and stone buildings with cast-iron doors and shutters were able to survive fire. Every town from Mokelumne Hill to Angels Camp had its story of rising from the ashes after devestation.

MY FIRST SUMMER LIVING FULL-TIME in the country was marked by scorching heat that hit 110 degrees. Soft ochre dirt burned my bare feet, and the smell of pine pitch filled the air with a faint turpentine scent. Early one Friday morning, I hiked down to the creek on a fire road that had been cut during the Old Gulch fire of 1991, hoping for a trickle of water. No such luck. Even wild mint that had grown abundantly the previous spring had dried up. On the return trip, sweaty T-shirt sticking to the skin on my back, I caught sight of a manzanita limb encrusted with red clay lying by the side of the trail. Squatting down, I dug it out of the earth with a sharp rock, uncovering a two-pronged branch that looked like the antlers of a mythical creature.

After lunch, I cleaned it up. Scrubbing away a decade of dirt and ash with a wire brush revealed a magnificent surface. This piece of wood had survived a fire that reduced thousands of acres of forestland to a charred moonscape. Intense heat brought sap to the surface, varnishing the wood like fine old furniture. As I polished it to a deep purple patina with steel wool, the image of an ibex began to form in my mind, a large wild goat with long curved horns that lives in the mountains of North Africa, Asia, and Europe.

Learning from the process of creating my dad's trilogy, every mask I made from then on would be sculpted over a life mask of my face, providing a base for the work and leaving my "signature" imprinted on the inside. For the ibex, I constructed a wire scaffolding to hold the horns in place, formed aluminum foil in the shape of the head, and sculpted the finished piece using papier-mâché. I textured the dry surface with a coarse metal file to suggest hair and painted it. When I held the ibex up to my face and looked into the mirror, I saw an animal spirit of survival and transformation.

Chapter 11

I MET GEORGE AT THE END OF MY ten-year marriage. The year 2000 had dawned. Our computers hadn't crashed on December 31, and the world as we knew it hadn't come to an end. I reminded myself that I hadn't crashed either. It was the new millennium, and I was ready for a new beginning.

We were introduced by a mutual friend, Judith, who encouraged me by saying, "You and George both have barns, and you're artists. I think you should meet." The divorce was final and the dust had settled. I had my freedom and nothing much left to lose. The "barns" my friend referred to were our studios. George's was in the middle of a rose garden.

Judith and I drove from Berkeley to Petaluma on a gorgeous spring day. So many shades of green were vibrating in the sunlight, it felt as if I were hallucinating green in the shapes of trees, gardens, and fields of grass dotted with cows. Twenty minutes out of town, we turned into a driveway. Spread out before us was a vast field of roses, acres of rosebushes blooming in shades of pink, red, yellow, and orange. The scent was intoxicating. We followed a narrow path to a small wooden building with a shed roof. Judith shouted, "Hey, George! We're here!" A man of medium build with a full beard and thinning hair down to his shoulders came out to greet us. He was wearing old jeans with a patina of dried oil paint. He and Judith hugged, delighted to see each other. I stood back, enjoying their friendship. George turned toward me and nodded approvingly. I said, "I think I see a hug coming." It was like shaking hands, only friendlier.

On a large easel in a corner of his studio was a painting George had been working on. It captured my attention, the Golden Gate Bridge with cars streaming across and two joggers running alongside. George invited me to check out his website while he and Judith caught up. I thought, *Hmmm . . . the guy wants to impress me.*

I learned that he'd been painting cityscapes for twenty-five years on just about every street corner in San Francisco, "capturing the energy of The City like no one else had." At some point, he said casually, "I just finished a short promo video I'd like you to see." It started with George crossing the Golden Gate Bridge on his motorcycle, with a French easel strapped on the back. The soundtrack shifted from rock to cool jazz as the artist set up his easel on a corner in the Marina District with a Starbucks in the background. I could feel the constant movement of people as his subjects came to life on the canvas.

The three of us went to lunch at a Thai restaurant in Petaluma, and George told me that he had come full circle in San Francisco. He was searching for something new. We were both in transition. I respected him as an artist and enjoyed his company. We became friends, and then lovers.

OUR FIRST REAL DATE WAS A WEEKLONG motorcycle ride to Washington State. We'd been seeing each other for a few weeks when George said, "I'm going to Seattle next month. Why don't you come with me?" He'd grown up in Tacoma and left home when he was fourteen. He told me that he had never visited the graves of his father, mother, and older brother, and it felt like time. The last time I'd ridden a motorcycle was my own Yamaha street bike when I was twenty, but I thought, *Why not?* The journey was a shared adventure. It's amazing what you can learn about a man when you're riding behind him on a motorcycle for 1,500 miles. We started spending weekends together at my place in Mountain Ranch, and when I made the decision to move there full-time, George moved with me.

We were two creative adults engaged in parallel play, each in our own sandbox. We worked alone. We had different friends and, except for our work as artists, different interests. I did what I wanted, as did George. We never asked for permission. The glue that held our relationship together was art.

I needed freedom and got it, in my life and in my relationship with George. My real love affair was with the natural world. Walking the trails through every season, listening to the wind and coyotes howling in the night, bonding with the land and its creatures, I discovered that being alone did not mean loneliness. I began to feel part of the life all around me and to find myself in my art form. It ignited my curiosity and imagination. I read everything I could find about mask-making, mask-dancing, and mask ritual. I saw material for masks wherever I looked— in feathers and bones, tree fungus, rusty bottle caps, and the carcasses of insects. In a frenzy of inspiration, everything I touched seemed to come to life, in one mask after another.

George rediscovered an earlier love for landscape painting *en plein air*, French for "in the open air." He would leave before the sun came up, tossing his French easel into the back seat of his car along with a tackle box of oil paints, brushes, and turpentine. When he came home at dusk, tired and satisfied, I could see the river, meadow, or ancient oak tree he had painted through his eyes. Our relationship was working well for both of us.

OVER THE NEXT FIVE YEARS, I was represented by a few local galleries, with shows in Berkeley and San Francisco and a group show at Artexpo in New York City. George's landscapes were featured at a gallery in Reno, and we did a show together in the Marina District. Neither of us liked the amount of time that marketing our work took away from doing our work. We realized that we needed our own venue. One Sunday morning, we had just finished brunch at the Murphys Hotel, deep in conversation about this, when I glanced across the street and saw a For Rent sign in the historic Cheap Cash Store. Built in 1860, it was a beautiful stone building with tall ceilings, upstairs loft, and an office in back with a bathroom. I made an appointment to meet with the landlord the following Friday. I signed a one-year lease that very day. In less than a week, we had our venue.

The Art Gallery in Murphys was scheduled to open a month later. After four weeks of furious remodeling and painting the front doors red, we were hanging our art for the grand opening when a couple came in and bought two of my masks. It felt like a good omen. During the previous decade, Murphys had become a tourist destination for people wanting to escape the congestion and fast pace of the Bay Area. This small town in Calaveras County was perfect. Now we could make, show, and sell our art our own way. It seemed as if George and I had a common sandbox, and we could become more intimately involved in each other's lives.

Chapter 12

THE IBEX MASK WAS THE BEGINNING of my series *Faces of Nature*. I learned that found objects, especially those in nature, have inherent power. A bone bleached white, with honeycomb interior, became a mask of timelessness. A butterfly wing with a stained-glass pattern in orange, yellow, and blue inspired a delicate filigree mask with silken wings. I made a Picassoesque clown face from fragments of abalone shell with iridescent swirls of purple, silver, and green. Then a second series ignited in my mind. What if I used the ritual of the mask to explore the relationship between creativity and spirituality?

I left the Christian community around the time I moved to Berkeley, hungering for a spiritual practice that was not part of a particular religion but that would speak to a shared humanity. I explored various forms of meditation and was drawn to chakra meditation because it focused on the relationship between mind and subtle energies in the body. I saw the seven energy centers (chakras) as a symbolic structure connecting mind, body, and spirit. The purpose was balance and the free flow of energy up and down the spinal cord from the first chakra at the base of the spine, grounding human experience on the earth, to the seventh chakra at the crown of the head, representing our connection with the infinite. At the center was the heart chakra, the longing to love and be loved. From base to crown, each of the seven chakras expressed its own energy. One flowed into the other, from survival needs to sexuality, personal power to love, communication to intuition, culminating in our relationship with the universe.

The *Seven Chakras* series was a year in the making. Life presented me with experiences expressing the energy of each chakra. I was living what I was learning, and my creative work could not have been more personal. I will tell you the stories of the first chakra and the last. Since the first chakra is about grounding human experience to the earth, I asked myself what my experience of the earth was here and now.

ON MARCH 19, 2003, I DROVE TO a studio I had in town in my aging, four-wheel-drive Subaru, bouncing from one rut to another down the dirt road from my house. Green hills undulated like enormous ocean swells, dotted with early orange poppies and purple lupin. Spring was so close I could feel it in the air. But I also felt a collective sense of fear, building for months, fueled by the unrelenting media coverage leading up to the United States' invasion of Iraq. Strident voices chanted anti-terrorist slogans and made frightening projections about Iraq's weapons of mass destruction. How could I indulge in the joy of spring and make a mask that only celebrated the earth's renewal? I needed to go into the darker recesses of the spirit.

Eighteen months after 9/11, images of the Twin Towers erupting in flames with malignant gray smoke billowing up into a blue sky, still lingered in everyone's mind. A sense of helplessness, rage, and grief reverberated across the United States as we prepared to wage a "War on Terror." My fear also triggered disturbing memories from childhood. Among the most terrifying were learning to "duck and cover" during the

Cold War era and the fear of a nuclear war between the Soviet Union and the United States.

It is 1950. I am six years old, huddled under my desk like a turtle with no shell, knees up to my chin, hands cupping the back of my head. My first-grade classmates and I have been instructed to do this to protect ourselves from imploding glass and collapsing walls in the event of a nuclear attack. We do what we're told, staying still and quiet until the warning siren stops wailing.

For years, I would have nightmares of being very small and running with other children to find cover in a playground while airplanes flew overhead dropping bombs.

Driving to my studio five decades later, I realized that I had relegated this particular fear to childhood, so that I could live my adult life in denial about it ever happening again. The reality of 9/11, and the buildup to a military revenge, had eaten through my denial like acid. I needed to channel my fear, grief, and rage into art that was relevant to this time but that would also transcend it.

The first chakra mask had revealed herself to me as I walked the land. I saw her in the sunburned earth of summer, inlaid with small stones and tiny quartz crystals, in butterfly wings, tangled vines, feathers, and bits of bleached animal bones. But when I spread my collection out on the worktable, questions assaulted me. What was true? What was honest? Was my responsibility as an artist to create an ideal image or one that was real? In that moment, I knew that I could not sculpt a face of the earth at peace without including the reality of war, so I added other materials: spent ammunition; burnt wood; charred roots; rusted barbed wire; a green-and-black bull's-eye target with the center blown open; my children's teeth, stolen from the tooth fairy; and curls of their baby hair. I was ready.

I shaped the left side of Earth Mother's face from clay mixed with red earth: her nose, mouth, forehead, high cheekbones, and ear curved like a shell. Her eye was closed as if in sleep. Fragments of the living earth found their way into creases, an eyebrow, eyelashes, and hair. The right side was completely different. I pounded charcoal into powder and kneaded it into the clay to make her face ashen. Shell casings pockmarked her skin. A target encircled her right eye, and her mouth drooped like a stroke victim's. Dead roots became ragged hair.

As I looked at Earth's disfigured face, my throat tightened. I could hardly breathe. I wanted to escape. When I embedded my children's baby teeth and hair in the ash, I started to cry. *No. Not the children.* I was crying from my eyes, nose, and mouth. It felt like all life on Earth was crying. Then the anguish stopped, as abruptly as it had begun. What if, just for a moment, we all stopped? What if, suddenly, we realized the horror of what we were doing?

After creating the *Earth* chakra mask, every couple of months another door opened. Each mask had its own distinct story. At the end of the year, it was time for the seventh and final mask, Infinite Wisdom. What could I bring to this chakra that would evoke what unifies us?

I grew up in a family where the existence of God was not denied. God was just irrelevant. We were raised in a kind of cultural unbelief. But on Sunday mornings, when our parents wanted to be alone, my brother and I, four and eight years old, were sent on a bus to Sunday school at the Full Gospel Tabernacle. Although my cousin's grandfather was the preacher, we were forbidden to stay for the church service. I learned later it was because they spoke in tongues.

Fast-forward nine years. Our parents were getting a divorce. My brother and I were at an adult church service for the first time. Sitting side by side in a pew at the First Christian Church of Christ in our neighborhood, we felt embarrassed by our ignorance of protocol. We watched what other people did and followed along. We stood when they stood, found the right song in the hymn book when the music director told us where to look, and prayed at the appropriate times. We were doing OK until two silver trays were passed down the aisle with little round crackers on one and small cups of grape juice on the other. The minister said that the crackers represented the body of Jesus and the grape juice his blood. We should partake in remembrance of him. This was incomprehensible to us, so we passed the trays along.

I don't remember exactly why we went to church on that particular Sunday, but in my seventeenth year, in the midst of my parents' ugly divorce, I felt the need to know more about God. I believed that different religions were like different languages speaking about the same mystery. I reasoned that if I didn't learn at least one of them, I would be left with the uncertainties of my parents' beliefs and of life in general.

I stayed in the Christian church for thirty years. Although my husband and I went to church with our children and my kids were raised with the core values of Christian teaching, I questioned what other believers seemed to take for granted. I read the Bible through twice, seeking essential truths that could inform my life, and learned to pray in a way that was authentic for me. I accepted Jesus as my savior, with reservations. I listened to sermons preached by men of God. I baked casseroles for church gatherings. I served on boards of deacons. I loved the people in my Christian community. And all the time I knew that the Christian language was only one among many. A part of me felt like someone trying to pass as a Christian until I no longer could. When I left the church family that had welcomed me when I was seventeen, I became a spiritual orphan looking for a safe place to call home. But I was ready to experience a world filled with spiritual diversity.

TWENTY YEARS LATER, THE GENESIS of the seventh mask, Infinite Wisdom, was an image of great wings whose feathers were made of words of love and peace from sacred texts of people all over the world. I wanted to embrace Christians and pagans, Jews and Muslims, Hindus and Buddhists, to bring their essential teachings into my art. I tore out pages from my personal bibles, the Old and New Testaments and Gnostic Gospels, from copies of the Tao Te Ching, Bhagavad Gita, and *Zen Mind, Beginner's Mind*. I cut feather shapes from the pages and glued them to the wings unsegregated, painting each one in translucent, jewel-like colors so the words showed through. Beneath the wings was an ageless face with skin of gold leaf. A bird skull, symbol of life and death, completed the headpiece.

A verse from Ecclesiastes came to mind: "For everything there is a season for every purpose under heaven, a time to be born and a time to die . . . a time to love and a time to hate, a time for war and a time for peace." The seventh chakra mask became a prayer for the wisdom to live together in peace.

Chapter 13

I'D LEFT THE CHURCH IN MY FORTIES, increasingly intolerant of being relegated to a relationship with the divine in which I was a perennial child, seeking the favor of a heavenly father through the intercession of a perfect brother. On a simple human level, the inherent inequalities in this religious family system were obvious. In Catholic circles, even Mary, the mother of God, is relegated to fourth place. But I never lost an intimate connection with the Holy Spirit, dwelling in every human being, especially when I learned that she was female.

I was not interested in replacing a male god with a female one. But in my curiosity to learn what life was like when women had power in pre-patriarchal cultures, I discovered books by women researching and writing about the civilizations of the Goddess.

For thousands of years, before patriarchal systems became dominant, communities of people honored the sacred female and lived in harmony with nature. Contemporary archeologists, most notably Marija Gimbutas, digging down into the debris of human history, found at the bedrock people who worshipped the deity in female form as Maiden, Mother, and Crone. In Turkey, Old Europe, Malta, and Minoan Crete, cultures developed with systems of religious practice, language, law, visual arts, agriculture, mathematics, and commerce. What was most significant was what was absent: weapons of war.

If there were people who lived together without waging war, then perhaps it was not inherently "human nature" for people to kill one another. We cannot go back in time, but couldn't we go forward with a renewed vision of what might be humanly possible? *The Feminine Face of God* series began with this question, and two masks from the Judeo-Christian tradition: Shekhinah and Eve.

IT WAS A TYPICAL SATURDAY AT THE Art Gallery in Murphys, during a lull in the flow of tourists, when two parish priests walked in, looking out of place in their white collars and somber black cassocks. I had been trying to envision Shekhinah, the feminine indwelling spirit of God, and was stuck. How does one create an image of the ineffable? I thought, *Now's my chance. Not one, but two Catholic priests! Who better to have this conversation with?* I smiled and said, "Welcome to our gallery. Is this your first time here?" They answered yes and looked around rather uncomfortably at the array of mask faces staring at them.

I said, "I'm the artist, and this is my work. I've been working on a new series entitled *The Feminine Face of God* and wanted to know more about Shekhinah. I understand that she's a feminine manifestation of God. Can you tell me more about that?"

They got a deer-in-the-headlights look, avoiding my searching gaze.

One cleared his throat and said quietly, "We don't talk about that."

He turned abruptly toward the door, followed by his fellow priest, and made a hasty exit. Wow. It seemed obvious to me that I was on the right track.

The priests' reaction gave me insight into how powerful Shekhinah was. I sculpted a strong face, bone-white, and shaped clay to form the points of a star that spun out from her third eye, the center of intuition. While the clay was still wet, I placed small pieces of broken tile in chakra colors, red, orange, yellow, green, blue, indigo, and purple, at the tips of each point to catch the light. This is the poem I wrote for her:

SHEKHINAH

In the beginning they said
God created man in His own image
Male and female
He created them

But where am I
A woman looking into the mirror
Provided by God the Father
I see no reflection of myself

The Mother of my soul is not there
Not in a woman born from Adam's rib
Not in a virgin giving birth
Ignorant of her own sexuality

Like a girl child
Always on the outside
Looking in the window of my religion
I find no doorway

Like a hungry woman
I search in widening circles
Outside patriarchal boundaries
For spiritual food

And then I find Her waiting
At the center
In the beginning was Shekhinah
The Feminine Face of God

The Eve mask followed, face the color of warm earth, sensual and knowing, with full lips. Her right hand cupped her chin in a gesture of contemplation. She held a rosary of cowrie shells, which in many ancient cultures are considered to represent the vagina. A small silver icon, the biological symbol for female, dangled from its base. Apple seeds circled her third eye. Eve's poem reinterprets the Genesis narrative:

Eve

I am
She
Who first
Tasted
The fruit of
Knowledge
One bite
And
I knew
Good
And evil as
Choices

Ah, serpent
Symbol
Of power
You
Were my first
Partner

Without
Our
Dialogue
Humanity
Would dwell in
Paradise

Ignorant
Of
The magnificent
Terror
Of
Possibility

How was it possible to have been born female, a girl growing up, a woman coming of age, only knowing a male image of the divine? I had little conscious knowledge of what was missing. Like a strange fish swimming in a patriarchal ocean, I could not detach sufficiently to see why I didn't fit.

Creating Shekhinah and Eve enabled me to separate, to see, to think deeply and ask questions for myself. Feasting on images and stories of the Goddess, I found inspiration. Faces of the goddess began to fill my gallery walls, the Black Madonna, Kuan Yin, Athene, Kali, Medusa, the Crone, the Sleeping Goddess, Gaia, providing guidance in understanding my journey as a woman.

Chapter 14

IN 2011, AT THE AGE OF SIXTY-SEVEN, I walked part of the ancient trail that Tibetan traders traveled to trade salt for grain in the marketplace of Namche Bazaar in Nepal. The last leg of my journey started at Namche and ended in the village of Gokyo, at 17,000 feet. That experience changed my life in ways I could not have imagined three years earlier, when I first began to feel drawn to the Himalayas and the highest mountain in the world.

It began in such an ordinary way, on a spring afternoon in Berkeley. I was spending the weekend with my friend Carolyn, having a cappuccino at Peet's Coffee. During a break in our conversation, I glanced down at a Sunday edition of the *San Francisco Chronicle* that someone had left on the table next to us. When I picked it up, the Travel section fell out. An iconic photo of Mount Everest on the front page caught my attention. The feature article was about trekking in Nepal. I held it out to Carolyn and said, "Look at this—people trekking in the Himalayas. You don't have to climb a mountain and die!" I tore the article out of the paper and stuffed it into my jeans pocket, feeling a secret, almost forbidden, sense of excitement. That possibility became a kind of private enchantment. It lodged somewhere in my mind, circling around a deeper longing I couldn't name.

Later that year, I met Keith, a consummate musician, composer, and a man who loved going into the Sierra Nevada for a month at a time with a backpack filled with coffee, oatmeal, beans, and not much else. It was a quiet Saturday night at the Art Gallery in Murphys, just Keith and me hanging out. Keith was strumming his guitar, noodling around, when I thought, *Yosemite is Keith's second home. I'm going to ask him for advice.* I wanted to backpack in the Sierra and had recently bought a tent, down sleeping bag, backpack, bear box, and hiking boots. I'd asked some of my outdoorsy women friends if they would go with me, but there were no takers, so I made up my mind to go alone. I had just turned sixty-five and wanted to honor that milestone by climbing Half Dome.

Yosemite was a two-hour drive from my home. Trekking in Nepal was halfway around the world. Yosemite seemed like a good place to start. When I told Keith my plan, he looked at me and said, "Why don't you go with me?"

"Really?"

"Yeah."

"But I haven't backpacked in a long time."

"No problem."

"No problem? That's incredible! Yes, let's do it!" We made a date to go the next weekend.

We left on Friday, after the gallery closed, and drove in Keith's old van down Highway 120 to Groveland, a town near the eastern entrance of Yosemite National Park. We stopped for pizza. It was getting late when Keith said, "I know a place where we can sleep for the night and go into the valley as soon as the sun's up." The place was off the highway on a dirt road, in a grove of oak trees. No one else was around. We spread our sleeping bags on the ground, and I lay awake half the night while Keith snored like a hibernating bear. Although the moon was full and I was too excited to sleep, I must have dozed, because Keith woke me up while it was still dark, saying, "Get up. It's time to go."

The entrance checkpoint wasn't open yet, so we cruised right in, grabbed an egg burrito in the village, and stood in a line that was already twenty people long to get a permit to camp at the base of Half Dome. I had my heart set on climbing Half Dome. It would be my first time. When we got to the desk, the ranger said all the permits were taken for the entire weekend. I was crestfallen. Keith took one look at my face and said, "You really want to go."

"Yeah."

"OK. Let's get going. We've got to haul ass if we're going to do this in one day. It's already ten o'clock."

After leaving our backpacking gear in the van, we caught a tram to the trailhead, incongruously named Happy Isle. We shouldered our daypacks, mine filled with a bag of nuts, some trail mix, a few granola bars, a couple of oranges, a water bottle, and a sweatshirt. It was a glorious late-summer day, warm, the air scented with the pungent smell of pine sap. Keith said, "We've got a sixteen-mile round trip ahead of us. It's going to be dark by eight. You sure you want to do this?"

"Yes!" I said, grinning in blissful ignorance. I felt as if I could sprint all the way up the John Muir Trail.

I loved the freedom of hiking without the weight of a full-size pack, following Keith, finding my own rhythm, arms swinging along with the cadence of each step. By noon it was hot, and I welcomed any shade that fell across the trail, any outcropping of rock to sit on. We zigged and zagged along switchbacks, stopping to rest at Clark Point. Forget sprinting. At this point, I was trudging up the mountain, determined not to disappoint myself or Keith. No matter what, we were going to climb Half Dome.

We reached the base at about three o'clock and stopped, literally to catch our breath. We had ascended nearly five thousand feet in five hours. Gulping water and devouring handfuls of trail mix, I mentally prepared to climb the monolithic dome, glistening in the afternoon sun. It looked like the hump of a gigantic landlocked whale. First, we had to climb a flight of granite stairs, find a pair of grubby gloves in a basket next to the steel cable handrails, and get in line. Ahead of me, I saw what looked like a colony of human ants going up and down a pathway that went straight up the whale's back. It was about four feet wide, with metal fence posts embedded into the rock to hold the cables. Flimsy-looking two-by-fours were secured across the trail as footholds, presumably to prevent someone from sliding down four hundred feet to her death. My heart was beating so hard it felt audible. My mouth was dry as dust. Then it was my turn. I looked back to be sure that Keith was right behind me, feeling sweat running down the sides of my thin T-shirt. I was scared. The first step was the hardest. My legs felt shaky. The muscles in my arms and hands were already tense. I took a second step and then a third, driving myself to override the fear. *Grip the cables. Hold on. Do not look down. Brace your legs on the two-by-fours.* My feet felt prehensile in my boots, trying to grip the hard surface. *Keep going.* Time was meaningless. The only reality was now.

Legs quivering, hands aching, I released the cables and stood on level ground. Every muscle in my body felt sore, but I had made it to the top. I got out of the way of people waiting in line to go down and stood very still, watching for Keith to summit. He gave me a big hug and said, "Congratulations!"

All I could say was, "Thank you, thank you, thank you," as I slowly spun around and around, taking in the 360-degree panorama of Yosemite Valley. We walked to the edge and looked down a sheer wall to the valley below, breathing in this place, this aliveness, this moment. And then we had to go down. It was getting late.

Descending seemed less traumatic, because we'd made it to the top. I backed down as I would have on a stepladder, and we found a secluded place to rest. Keith smoked a joint. I unwrapped a granola bar and munched quietly. We didn't talk. It was five o'clock and beginning to cool off. I put on my sweatshirt and we set off down the trail. We had eight miles to go.

The descent to Yosemite Valley was like a walking dream. Because we were tired, it was much harder going down. By the time we got to Clark Point, my knees were aching. Each step hurt. Encroaching darkness made it difficult to navigate switchbacks. By eight o'clock, a full moon began to rise above the distant mountains. We had such a long way to go. All we could do was keep walking. On steep parts of the trail, I had to walk backward to relieve the pain in my knees. At about midnight, Keith said, "We need to stop and rest." But where? He gestured to a flat spot just off the trail, big enough for the two of us. He lay down, resting his head on his arms, and was soon asleep. I curled into my body, trying to keep warm. I felt like a fox with no den, wary and hypervigilant. I had dozed and awakened several times, repeatedly startled by the sound of human feet just a few yards away, when Keith woke up and said, "Let's go." I sat up abruptly and heard a male voice scream, "Oh my God!" Seeing me, the hiker said, "I thought you were a mountain lion!" I felt curiously proud of myself and responded, "Sorry I scared you," as he ran away from me as fast as he could.

The night wore on as we made our way down the mountain on our own hero's journey. It had become mythical—and interminable. Early in the morning, before daylight, we saw a trail of pilgrims, seemingly hundreds of them with flashlights in hand on their way to Half Dome, snaking up the same trail we had walked just the day before. They obviously heeded the ranger's advice and had left way before the recommended 7 a.m. departure time. I smiled wearily at them and silently gave my blessing. We had trekked to Little Yosemite Valley, climbed Half Dome, and come back down, in one long, sixteen-hour day. We had done it, and I was proud.

Chapter 15

AT SIXTY-FIVE, MOST PEOPLE THINK about retirement and slowing down, but I was just hitting my stride. I had been on two magnificent journeys, one inward, the other out into the natural world. Opening to the "Mother of my soul" in creating *The Feminine Face of God* felt like a second birth, and I was the midwife. I remembered holding my youngest child an hour after she was born and seeing her eyes open in wonder. How incredible at my age to feel such soulful wonder—and hunger for food I had not yet tasted. After Half Dome, I went on other treks in the Sierra until my private enchantment to draw close to Mount Everest became an imperative.

On Thanksgiving Day 2011, departing from San Francisco International Airport, I flew halfway around the world, a woman alone, carrying everything I needed for a thirteen-day trek in my carry-on backpack. Before the plane touched down on Nepali soil, I could see Mount Everest shining in the afternoon sun, like a dream image. There was no one to greet me. An airport official pointed me to the money-exchange kiosk and ran interference to get me a reputable taxi ride to the Hotel Holy Himalaya. I arrived sleep-deprived and wired at the same time. I watched Al Jazeera news on television until

I fell into a ragged sleep. The next morning, I was jet-lagged but eager to throw myself into the teeming life I had seen from my taxi window on the drive to the hotel.

On my first walk through the streets of Kathmandu, I felt bombarded by the frenzied energy of taxis, motorcycles, bicycles, rickshaws, and the occasional sacred cow, all going in opposing directions. There were no center lines, traffic signals, posted speed limits, or street signs. Drivers leaned into their horns to make their presence known. No one used seatbelts. At every intersection, it was a crapshoot to see who would get through first. And God help the pedestrians! All of this happened in a brown-gray cloud of smog. But in a strange way, the crazy motorized choreography seemed to work. This was only the second day of my trip, and I had yet to hear the wail of an ambulance, see a dead body in the street, or witness a car crash. It was truly astounding.

Somehow unscathed, I reached the center of Thamel, Kathmandu's tourist district, and was searching for a quiet spot to have a cup of tea when I found the "Garden of Dreams." From the street, all I could see was a high stucco wall that appeared to enclose an entire city block. At the entrance was a heavy carved wooden door, with a welcome sign in English. Pushing it open, I saw an expanse of green lawn, and in the distance a restaurant with outdoor tables. Perfect. The walls somehow kept out the stench and cacophony of the street. I breathed in the clean air and kicked off my sandals. Tossing them into a tote bag slung over my shoulder, I walked barefoot across the grass to the nearest table. I felt disoriented and exhausted from trying to get directions from passersby whose language I didn't speak, and my Lonely Planet guidebook was next to no help. A waiter in a white jacket came to take my order, asking, "Madam, what would you like?" in perfect English.

I responded, "Milk tea and a biscuit, thank you," relaxing for the first time since I had left Calaveras County.

My hotel was in the midst of shops that sold every type of trekking and climbing gear imaginable, in addition to soft pashmina scarves in rainbow colors, tea, spices, brass elephants, figurines of Buddhas and Hindu deities, sounding bowls, and glittering jewelry. I was surprised to find that Kathmandu also had bookstores with books in many languages, including English. I bought a used copy of *Cave in the Snow* , about Tenzin Palmo, an English woman my age who had come to Nepal to study Tibetan Buddhism when she was eighteen. She made a vow to attain enlightenment in female form no matter how many lifetimes it took, and she lived alone in a cave in the mountains for twelve years, three of those in strict meditation. I thought, *That's my kind of woman.* She broke the rules for a proper Englishwoman and dedicated her life to what she believed in. Although I had no desire to live in the Himalayas for a decade, and certainly not in a cave, reading the book was encouragement on my journey. I would carry it with me all the way on my fifty-mile trek.

DAY THREE IN KATHMANDU WAS entirely different. I awakened early and walked down a street that snaked into the shadows of a neighborhood market. It felt like a separate world. The smells were pungent and earthy. Fresh vegetables spilled out from baskets and boxes. There were mounds of orange and yellow fruit, pale green lentils in open bags, and freshly butchered goats, chickens, and fish. And no one paid attention to me. No one called out, endearingly or desperately, for me to buy their wares. I wandered alone, as if I were backstage, watching a performance I had no part in. As a tourist passing through, I knew I didn't belong there, but it didn't feel intrusive, because I was invisible. It was important that I return to my hotel by midafternoon, so I crossed the imperceptible border back into Thamel to look for a place to have lunch. This was the day I would meet my woman guide, Kanchi Sherpa.

Three Sisters, the only woman-owned trekking company in Nepal, had emailed instructions before I left the States. Kanchi would meet me in my hotel lobby at 4 p.m., accompanied by a representative from Three Sisters who would collect $861, the balance of my payment due. Kanchi could not take the money herself because we were leaving at 5:30 the next morning, and she wouldn't have enough time to make the deposit.

I arrived back at my hotel at 3 p.m., so I would have plenty of time to freshen up and greet my guide in the lobby. As I started up the stairs, someone called my name. I turned toward the voice and saw a woman dressed in a simple patterned skirt and blouse, with a weathered face and strong features. She wore no makeup, but her short hair was dyed magenta red. She looked about forty years old. Even halfway up the stairs, I could see the deep frown lines between her eyebrows, and I knew this was Kanchi. She was alone, and she was angry. I walked back down the stairs, trying to form an apology in my mind but not knowing what I needed to apologize for. In her heavily accented English, Kanchi told me that she had been waiting for three hours. The trekking company had told her I would be there at noon. Had I misunderstood our appointment time? Was I still in a jet-lagged fog and just screwed up? This wasn't how I wanted us to meet. I was afraid she would think I was a spoiled, entitled American woman who cared nothing for her time. Her English was rudimentary and my Nepali nonexistent, but we tried to figure out what had gone wrong and what to do next. We didn't even know each other, and already we had a huge cultural gap to bridge.

Kanchi called Three Sisters on her cell phone to report that their money courier had not arrived. Although I only heard half of the conversation, I could tell it was heated. The solution was for me to go with Kanchi in a taxi to a travel agency before it closed and leave the cash with the agent. We sat together in frustrated silence in the back seat of the cab, on a hair-raising ride through Kathmandu during rush hour. In that moment I felt despair. The gap between us seemed unbridgeable, two women from different generations without a common language. What had I done?

Once the money was paid, Kanchi directed the driver to drop me off at my hotel and told me to be ready at 5 a.m. We had a plane to catch. I hoped the clerk at the desk understood my English well enough to call me at 4:30.

I could not sleep. Still wide awake at 2 a.m., I was unable to turn off in my mind the story of the disaster of our first meeting. And we were leaving Tribhuvan Airport for the trailhead, Lukla, in just three and a half hours.

Chapter 16

AT 6 A.M. THE DOMESTIC TERMINAL AT the airport was nothing like the international terminal. The place was a cavernous warehouse filled with locals, tourists, and trekkers milling about in mass pandemonium. There were no electronic boards with flight information. I followed Kanchi as closely as I could without taking her hand. She plopped me down on a wooden bench between a Tibetan monk in a maroon robe and a Sherpa woman with a young child asleep in her lap, and she disappeared. Trying to focus on something, I pulled out my Lonely Planet guidebook and looked up "Air Travel." I read, "Nepal has an excellent network of domestic flights . . . however, pilots must still find their way using visual navigation . . . and few years pass without some kind of plane crash in the mountains." I had never been afraid of flying, but this gave me pause. When I looked up, Kanchi was standing in front of me saying, "Mama, come." This was the first time she had called me Mama. She told me that in her culture, this was a term of respect for older women. In the midst of all the chaos and confusion, I felt some hope that Kanchi was seeing me, and addressing me, for who I was. It was an important beginning for both of us.

I settled my backpack onto my shoulders and fastened the strap at my waist, so it rested on my hips, grasping the trekking poles I had bought in Kathmandu. We walked out onto the tarmac to board a very small airplane, along with ten other passengers, for the forty-five-minute flight. We had only one stewardess. Dressed in traditional Sherpa clothing, she wore a long, elegant sheath dress called an *engi* with a simple, striped apron, a *metil*. As soon as we were airborne, she passed out cotton balls for our ears and a piece of hard candy to suck on. We began our gradual ascent to Lukla Airport, at 9,000 feet. Below me, I could see green concentric circles of terraced land under cultivation. Then, abruptly, it was very steep. The plane did not seem to slow down to land. Later, I'd only recall freeze-frames in rapid succession: a green landscape at a ninety-degree angle, an absurdly short runway flanked by tiny houses, and at the end of the runway, a huge slab of mountain. It felt like trying to land a plane on Lombard Street in San Francisco.

Over a breakfast of Sherpa pancakes at a café owned by one of her relatives, Kanchi told me Lukla was the most dangerous airport in the world. A flight she was on when she was pregnant with her first-born child had crash-landed on the runway. No one was hurt. She said this without emotion, but with deep seriousness. I put my hand gently on hers across the table. It was the first personal information she'd shared with me.

After finishing breakfast, we paid our bill and walked through town to the trailhead, assuming what would be our pattern for the next two weeks. Kanchi, the guide, took the lead. She was lean, with the easy stride of a girl who grew up tending sheep in these mountains, walking these dirt paths. The day was warm, and she wore lightweight tan hiking pants, the kind with big pockets in front and back, loose, so she could move freely. A red and olive-green patterned scarf, tied in the back, covered her hair. In a couple of blocks, the asphalt became dirt. It was noon on the first day of our thirteen-day trek. Destination: Gokyo Ri.

I was happy just walking this trail. Life was simple. I thought, *I can do this. Put one foot in front of the other. Breathe. Take the next step. Breathe. Follow Kanchi Sherpa. Stop to rest. Drink water. Stop for a lunch of dal bhat and sweet, hot Nepali tea with milk*. This was walking meditation. I lost track of time. As the sun began to slip behind jagged, snow-covered mountain peaks, we arrived at our first "teahouse," the sturdy, two-story home of a Sherpa family who offered a hot meal and narrow bed in a small room with unpainted plywood walls for about $10. We ate dinner with the mother and her four grown children at a table near the woodstove. I could hardly keep my eyes open, so I said good night early and went to bed.

In the middle of the night, I woke up abruptly, smelling burning wood. I thought, *The mother is up early making breakfast*, but then sensed that something was wrong. I heard her urgent voice in the adjacent room where her children slept. "Get up. Get up! There's a fire in the kitchen!" She wasn't speaking English, so how did I know what she was saying? It was so dark that I could barely see my hiking boots on the floor next to the bed. I remembered putting my flashlight in one of them. Fumbling for it, I pushed the button, but it didn't work. I pulled on my jeans in the dark, shoved my feet into the boots, and felt my way down the outside stairs. The only illumination was a single yard light. I found the mother in the kitchen with her daughters. Her son was focused on removing smoking pieces of wood from around the woodstove. The fire was still burning somewhere and he was trying to find its source. I sat in silence on a bench with the two younger daughters. We watched as their brother pulled out a twisted, blackened electrical wire. A small flame leaped up the wall. The oldest girl poured water on it to put it completely out.

We smiled at each other in shared relief. The mother turned to me, holding the burned cord, and said emphatically, in English, "Dangerous!" My eyes teared up as I told her, "I am grateful your house is safe." I wasn't sure she understood my words, but I hoped she felt my empathy. Climbing back up the stairs to bed, I wondered why Kanchi had not come down the stairs and into the kitchen, but it was too late to investigate. In three hours, we would begin our climb to Namche Bazaar. It would take the whole day to ascend to 11,286 feet.

In the morning over breakfast, I asked Kanchi where she had slept.

"In the big room."

"Where?"

"On the benches . . . where all guides sleep."

"But if there are men, are you the only woman?"

"Yes."

"Kanchi, I want you to have your own room. I can afford it." She looked at me, into my eyes. Then she said, "OK, Mama. Thank you."

I began to feel the pull of Mount Everest with growing anticipation, but I was uncomfortable using the name given by a British surveyor, Sir George Everest, as if the mountain could be claimed as a colonial possession. On our first rest break, I asked Kanchi what Sherpa people call the mountain. When she told me, "Chomolongma, the Great Mother," I realized that it was her call I had been hearing for three years. The Great Mother, manifested in her myriad forms, had inspired *The Feminine Face of God. Cho-mo-long-ma* became my silent mantra. I chanted it in rhythm with my footsteps all the way to Namche Bazaar.

My breathing became more labored as we gained altitude, and at midday, we stopped. It seemed a miracle that two young girls were selling oranges by the side of the trail. I took one and peeled it greedily, savoring the sweet, tart taste. Kanchi said gently, "Mama, look up." I saw Chomolongma touching the heavens. At the highest point, a windswept cloud of snow looked like a wisp of her hair. I had no words, only tears. Kanchi asked, "This is your dream?"

I answered, "It is my heart opening."

I had come to Nepal knowing no one. I came alone, without cell phone, laptop, appointment book. No obligations. Without fully realizing it, I had begun training with Keith when we climbed Half Dome, and for months before boarding the plane for Kathmandu, I walked my land without missing a day. My intention was to trek from Lukla at 9,000 feet to Gokyo Ri at 18,000 feet, to meet Chomolongma. I came knowing that anything can happen in Nepal, because anything can happen in life. Never had I lived so fully in the moment.

AFTER SIX HOURS OF TREKKING, I was exhausted, still chanting *Cho-mo-long-ma* to myself, when I saw a white dome with a peaked top shining dully in the setting sun. This was the village stupa at the entrance to the town of Namche Bazaar, honoring Lord Buddha. It had become increasingly hard for me to breathe. Our water bottles were almost empty, and my lips felt dry and chapped. It was a great relief when Kanchi turned to me and said, "This is Namche. We can stop now."

Namche Bazaar is an important acclimation point for climbers and trekkers. It's imperative to stay in Namche at 11,000 feet for a minimum of three days, for one's lungs to learn to breathe the thin air. Altitude sickness could become a lethal danger the higher we climbed. This late in the season, there would be no medical help, save for a helicopter, and only if weather permitted.

We wound our way through the town of traditional Sherpa houses and family-owned businesses spread out in a horseshoe shape. At the center of the horseshoe was the bazaar. For centuries, merchants from Tibet had come every year to sell their wares. To make this journey, they traversed one of the highest mountain passes in the world. But this annual migration ended in 1950, when China invaded Tibet. Their ancestral home obliterated, the traders sought asylum in Nepal.

Eventually, we came to a large whitewashed two-story dwelling. A stocky middle-aged man smiled down at us through an open window. Kanchi said, "We will stay here." When we were introduced, I learned that he was Kanchi's brother-in-law, Ang Tshering. The door opened even before we could knock, and her sister, Dawa Futi, greeted us with polite reserve. Kanchi was home with her family, and I felt welcomed. It would be good to catch my breath here.

Dinner that night was served in the great room, a living room and dining room all in one. We had *momos*, little dumplings filled with greens from the garden, a delicious mushroom soup, and, of course, milk tea. Traditionally, foreign guests were served before the family, who took their meals in the kitchen. My dining companions were a French couple and a family of four from Israel, a mother, father, and two young adults on break from their university. The conversation was a stew of languages, but we asked one another in English, "Where are you from? Where are you going?" Although I loved the easy camaraderie among people traveling in a country not their own, I was getting accustomed to the solitude of solo trekking and missed Kanchi's quiet companionship. I longed to be in the kitchen. When it was just the two of us and a host family, meals were more informal.

The next evening at dinner, there were no other guests. Ang Tshering, the man of the house, and I were served first. On their television, we watched the news together, commenting on the similarities among politicians around the world. Although Nepal's first democratic elections had been held twenty years earlier, Nepal's king was not deposed until 2006.

Their experience of democracy was still in its formative stage. I learned that Ang Tshering had been a guide on numerous Everest summits and had been invited by Americans who had climbed with him to visit them in cities across the United States. He had even climbed Half Dome in Yosemite. I felt ridiculous pleasure in swapping Yosemite stories with the man who had guided the first successful Japanese ascent of Everest. At the same time, I felt conflicted. Before Europeans discovered the peak they named Everest, the Sherpa did not "conquer" these magnificent mountains, believing them to be the abodes of divine beings. I wondered what it was like for them now. Foreign climbing and tourism had become crucial to their livelihood. I had so many questions, but I didn't feel I knew Ang Tshering well enough to ask them without seeming to be presumptuous or judgmental.

In the afternoon on my third day of acclimatization in Namche, I felt so good and strong that I wanted to celebrate, and I imagined buying a special treat for dinner in the village. Somehow, Kanchi's family knew that I had not taken a shower since I had left my hotel in Kathmandu. Did I smell? In any case, they gave me the gift of a hot shower. Water was precious in these mountains. Although wild rivers flowed in the deep crevasses and valleys of the Himalayas, they were hard to access, and wood to heat the water was difficult to find. At high altitude where trees are sparse and stunted, only fallen wood was taken, and it had to be carried long distances on the backs of young men. I felt uncomfortable using these valuable resources for the pleasure of a shower, but I knew that it was important to receive their gift.

First, a fire was kindled in the wood-burning stove, filled with juniper limbs laid on top of scrap cardboard, to heat water in a small storage tank. It took about fifteen minutes while I waited, wrapped in a towel, in the concrete stall that was also used as a toilet. When Kanchi poked her head in and said it was time, I straddled the porcelain floor toilet, shampoo bottle in hand, and turned the faucet on. The rush of warm water felt exquisite. I turned the water off, shampooed quickly, and soaped down. After a second rinse, it was done. I had never felt so clean in my life. I dried off and donned clean clothes, thinking, *Now I'm ready for Gokyo Ri. Bring it on!*

At an altitude of 17,575 feet, it was my final destination, my personal summit, with a spectacular view of the Great Mother at sunrise. It would take three days. I had already come a long way. In no way did the fact that I was sixty-seven years old seem like an impediment.

Kanchi was less sanguine. Concerned about my lung capacity and stamina, she wanted to err on the side of caution. People die from altitude sickness. The early symptoms are difficulty breathing, fatigue, headache, loss of appetite, nausea, and vomiting. To survive, you must descend to a lower altitude, and you can never go to sleep at the altitude where you became symptomatic. So, at the eleventh hour, Ang Tshering looked for a porter to carry my day pack from Namche to Gokyo and back. He found Gopal, a quiet, stocky young man with limited English and a shy smile. We were ready.

Chapter 17

FOR THREE DAYS WE HIKED above the timberline. Stark mountains towered over deep valleys. On the first day, the trail skirted the edge of a precipice, and I could hear the Dudh Kosi River far below, a torrential flood tumbling over ancient stones. Stone houses seemed to grow out of the rock on flat mesas. Because there was no timber, even fences and small barns were built of stone.

We spent the first night in Dole, the only guests. Our host was an artist who painted the landscape and animals that are part of Sherpa life and folklore, including yeti, the Himalayan bigfoot. Captivated by the stories brought to life in his direct, skillful style, I bought a small canvas. We rolled it up, and Gopal carried it in my pack.

Machhermo was the final stop before our ascent to Gokyo and the six sacred lakes that surround it. I slept fitfully, not knowing if I had mild altitude sickness or was simply antici-pating the last, most difficult challenge. *Whatever, I'm going.*

I woke up with the sun and got dressed. After a breakfast of hot porridge, white bread with honey, and milk tea, Kanchi shouldered her backpack. Gopal hefted both mine and his. I grabbed my trekking poles and we headed out, Kanchi in the lead, me in the middle, and Gopal bringing up the rear.

By late morning, the trail was a precarious path, barely wide enough for a human, let alone the occasional caravan of yaks. When a small herd came toward us, we could see the cloud of dust and smell them before they came into view, and we pressed our bodies against the mountainside. The huge, shaggy animals were burdened with all manner of supplies. I could hear them snorting and smell their rank breath as they lumbered within inches of us.

I took one step at a time, one breath at a time, silently chanting *Cho-mo-long-ma* to maintain focus. The higher we climbed, the harder it was to breathe, but I was OK as long as I kept up a slow, steady pace. I felt like a kid on a long vacation trip asking, "Are we there yet?"

Then I saw something both shocking and amazing, a wide gray staircase made of slabs of slate so steep it looked like a rough stone skyscraper. There was no mention of it in Lonely Planet, and we had not encountered anything like this before. I began to feel afraid for the first time, but I tried not to let it overwhelm me. There were no guardrails, but there had been none before. I took the first step, then the second, using my poles as two extra legs. On my left side was the mountain, on my right a sheer drop to the Dudh Kosi River, so far below it was a silver ribbon glistening in the noonday sun. *Do not look up. Do not look down. One step at a time. Cho-mo-long-ma. Cho-mo-long-ma. Cho-mo-long-ma. Just watch the step in front of you.* I was shaky and my steps were tentative. *Don't be scared. You've got to be strong. Keep going. One step at a time. Oh, fuck. I feel dizzy.* I moved slower and slower.

Gopal sensed something was wrong and came up behind me. "Gopal, I feel sick." I realized that there was no way I could turn around and go back down. *I am afraid. If I fall, I will die.* Gopal moved in close behind me, saying in a soft voice, "Slowly, slowly," like a soothing lullaby, "Slowly, slowly." I continued going up, one step at a time, steadying my body. It felt like dead weight on quivering legs. Clinging to the poles, I lifted myself up, straining with every muscle in my arms and across my shoulders.

Lungs gasping for the next breath, heart pounding, I prayed to reach Gokyo village. But as I summited, trying to steady myself on level ground, the high-altitude headache I feared began, squeezing the base of my skull and my forehead as if from the inside. There was no village in sight. By the time the first sacred lake came into view, a blue-green jewel in a forbidding setting, I was so fatigued that I could only move as an act of will. We plodded on. *One step, stop, breathe. One step, stop, breathe.* Finally, the village appeared in the distance. At the far end, we found a teahouse with a view of Gokyo Ri, my ultimate destination. It looked like a very tall lingam, the color of dirt.

I no longer cared. I just wanted to survive. I was too sick to go down, but there was no other option. There was no medical help, no helicopter.

Kanchi hoped food would revive me. I tried ginger tea and garlic soup, but I vomited after the first spoonful. Kanchi found a room for me and said she was going to find a horse to carry me down. I knew how to ride a horse, but I thought, *There's no way in hell I'm going down those stairs on a horse.*

I countered with, "I'm going to take ibuprofen first, wait a half hour, and then take a nausea pill. Let's see what happens." Inside, I was screaming, *I've got to walk down!* I lay stock-still on the cot. My head was throbbing, and I couldn't think. When I tried to lift it off the pillow, the dizziness hit hard in my head and my gut. I felt suspended in fear. What if there was no safe way down? After what seemed like an eternity, I sat up. My head wasn't spinning. My stomach felt hollow, but I was able to stand on shaky legs. *The medicine must be working.* It was getting dark, and we had to go down before nightfall. The three of us agreed that if I could not make it to the top of the stairs, we would stop wherever we were, and Gopal would go back to Gokyo and get a horse. As we headed across the high mountain plateau in the direction of the dreaded stairs, I felt spacey, as if I were in a bad dream that I couldn't wake up from, my head strangely disconnected from my body.

Then, out of nowhere, the French couple that we had met at Kanchi's family teahouse came running up to us, exclaiming, "*Bonjour*! How amazing to meet you again! Where have you been and where are you going?" They were just a day behind us. When we told them about my altitude sickness and that we had to go back without summiting Gokyo Ri, they were genuinely sympathetic. "Oh no! You've come so far. Is there any way we can help?" My answer was "No. Thank you. Remember me when you see Chomolongma at sunrise. Be safe." Their kindness gave me strength to keep going three more hours, slowly, slowly, down the slate stairs, and slowly, slowly, walking the yak trail back to the safety of Machhermo. Later, I'd have no memories of going down except putting one foot in front of the other: slowly, slowly.

FACING MORTALITY IS PART OF AGING. How was my trek in the Himalayas seven years earlier, a real, life-threatening experience, a metaphor for my inner journey? What comes to mind is a teaching from *The Tibetan Book of Living and Dying*: practice dying. It sounds paradoxical. How can one "practice dying" while living? What it means to me is to live each moment fully. This is how life gives its gift—one moment, one breath, at a time. Coming down the mountain, where I could breathe, where I was safe, felt like an ending as well as a beginning. The woman who had flown into Lukla Airport thirteen days earlier was not the same woman who returned. I knew who I was. I knew in my gut I could have died on that mountain. But who I was becoming had just begun to unfold.

Chapter 18

MY TREK IN NEPAL WAS NOT MY first pilgrimage. There'd been another, five years earlier. Then, too, I was trekking to an unknown place with five people I was just getting to know, in an aging school bus painted blue. I'd always wanted to go to Burning Man, and this year, the opportunity presented itself. A quote over the driver's seat from Che Guevara said, "Let us be realists . . . let us demand the impossible!" The interior was furnished with a cast-off sofa bed, an assortment of futons, a couple of deck chairs, and wooden cubbies that kids get in kindergarten. Four of us were musicians. Known as Clan Dyken, the Burning Man festival was their gig.

An assortment of guitars, a complete drum set, and a sound system were packed in black leatherette cases, stacked one on top of the other in the back of the bus, and bungeed so they wouldn't tumble down as we labored up Carson Pass on the way to Black Rock Desert. A borrowed trailer was hitched onto the back, with a ragtag assortment of bicycles. The bus would be our home for the next five days.

We were a motley crew of magnificent human beings, creative, passionate, gifted, necessarily flawed, each seeking our own enlightenment. Why else go to Burning Man? Catherine had sharp eyes that missed nothing and a mind that cut away any hypocrisy in herself or anyone else. She was quick to hug, to praise, to dance, to organize, to protect, and to love. We were the band's two groupies. Mark was a caregiver with a sensitive touch, whether with the skin of a drum, the steering wheel of a broken-down bus, or a frightened child. Bear was a poet and musician, with a righteous anger toward injustice. When Clan Dyken was on stage, everyone watched him, spellbound by his music. His partner was a beautiful young woman, long and lean, with cropped dark hair and guarded eyes. Somer was a talented singer overshadowed by Bear's charisma. And Bear's son, Silas, was balanced on the edge of manhood, his face in profile the mirror image of his father's. Music was the language they shared.

Where did I fit in? At a turning point in my life, I was an artist pushing against the boundaries of my own creativity, a woman on the cusp between middle and old age. I was at least a decade or two older than my companions. I had come to Burning Man seeking, paradoxically, both solitude and a connection to community not predetermined by my age.

After sleeping overnight on the shoulder of a side road off Highway 50, we woke up stiff and hungry, about an hour's drive from Fernley, Nevada, and the Black Bear Diner. It was time for breakfast. On our walk to the restaurant, I saw a sign in front of a Baptist church that admonished, "Hell, the ultimate Burning Man," and I knew I was going in the right direction. Black Rock Desert, the home of Burning Man, was just three hours away.

The sun was at its zenith when we drove off a two-lane highway onto a dirt road that snaked across the playa toward Black Rock City, rising out of the desert floor like a mirage. Our bus lumbered slowly behind a thousand other vehicles in a line of true believers heading toward Mecca. At the entrance, we produced our tickets to be scanned, as if they were passports. A bare-chested man wearing a pink tutu and combat boots poked his head into the bus searching for contraband: mind-altering drugs or other hallucinogenic substances (alcohol was OK), or "illegals" without tickets. Then he asked if there were any virgins. In unison, Catherine and Mark said, "Yeah, we have one," and pointed at me. I looked at them blankly. I was sixty-three years old, three times married, three times divorced with three kids, two stepkids, and an assortment of grandchildren. A virgin?

They laughed and said, "Go ahead. It's your initiation." This was only the first of many. I thought, *What the hell? Bring it on!* At the checkpoint I was invited to climb a scaffolding and straddle a bell that hung down between my legs. The bell was struck, resounding across the desert. I howled in abandon. Words from *Where the Wild Things Are*, which I read to my children when they were young, echoed in my mind: "Let the wild ruckus begin!"

IN THE MIDST OF SEEMING CHAOS, Black Rock City was laid out as if engineered. A semicircle of concentric streets defined where camps could set up. Straight streets, like the spokes of half a bicycle wheel, were thoroughfares that pointed toward The Man at the hub, an iconic, neon-lit figure atop an immense structure. Every year the design of the base changed to reflect a theme, but *The Man* did not. He has symbolized Burning Man since its inception on Baker Beach, San Francisco, on summer solstice 1986, and is always ritually immolated on Saturday night. We found the Musicians' Camp, and Mark introduced me to a few people hanging out in the shade of a huge tent. Mark and Catherine began to set up camp and told me to go explore.

The bikes weren't unloaded yet, so I walked out onto the playa, kicking up powdery dust with each step. The beat of electronic music was as ubiquitous as the heat. I was surrounded by people in continuous motion on bikes, riding weird vehicles, and walking; naked green people (this year's theme was "The Green Man"); women in S&M black leather with thigh-high boots; women wearing fairy wings and not much else; and others in sexy sequined dresses and stiletto heels. There were men dressed in tutus, some in makeup and elaborate wigs, and others dressed like X-rated pirates or deviant clowns.

On the playa, art cars cruised by looking like floating Rube Goldberg sculptures. I felt as if I were in a Fellini film with forty thousand other extras. The art—the magnificent, fantastical, irreverent, satirical, breathtaking art—was everywhere. I spun around, drunk on the art, the constant movement, the throbbing music, until I felt dizzy and had to stop, slowing down to a kind of vibrating stillness. I looked off toward the distant mountains and saw the most beautiful thing, the huge funnel of a dust devil dancing slowly across the desert. Totally enchanted, I thought, *How lovely.*

Moments later it was upon me. I was blinded by a total whiteout of swirling alkali particles. I hit the ground facedown and pulled my shirt up over my head. With nothing but a bra underneath, I wrapped my T-shirt around my face. Every inch of exposed skin felt sandblasted. Even time was stopped by the unrelenting force of the wind. All I could do was breathe through the dense filter of my shirt. Breathe and wait. Like a lizard caught out in the open by a predator, my body flattened against the warm earth, I lay absolutely still. Waiting.

A disembodied male voice above me asked, "Are you OK?"

"Yeah."

"You want a shirt for your back?"

"Yes, thank you."

I heard the crunch of his bike tires as he rode away. Dust filled every exposed orifice: ears, clenched eyes, nostrils, even my mouth. It tasted like some kind of dry, salty food. I waited. The wind was dying down when I heard the voices of a man and a woman. The woman said, "It's OK, you can get up now," and then they were gone.

When I rose and looked around, everything, including me, was covered in a fine patina of dust. The gift from a stranger lay at my feet, a military-green T-shirt with "U.S. ARMY" emblazoned across the front. I held it gratefully and surveyed this sun-scorched world. Although I only knew five people here, I felt like I belonged, and I realized that I needed to learn how to survive at Burning Man.

Catherine had told me to bring gallons of water, some food, sunscreen, dark glasses, a bike I didn't mind getting trashed riding around in the desert, a few clothes, my sleeping bag, and a journal. She said that if I forgot anything, I could probably find it in the stuff on the bus. I remembered shoving an unread pamphlet entitled "Survival Guide" in my backpack at the last minute before I left home. I needed to read it, *now*.

WALKING BACK INTO CAMP, I LOOKED like a desert rat that hadn't made it back to its hole before the storm hit. I expected everyone to say, "Oh my God! What happened to you?" A few of the musicians were sitting around talking. One guy was absently strumming his guitar, and a woman I met earlier looked up and said, "Hey." I felt invisible, as if camouflaged by my layer of alkali dust. Catherine and Mark were nowhere in sight. I climbed into the bus and flopped down on a futon. Guzzling water from a half-gallon jug, I began reading the "Survival Guide." I should have packed a dust mask and goggles to protect my eyes during dust storms, duct tape, a flashlight, first-aid kit, and "common sense, an open mind, sense of humor and a positive attitude." Man, was I totally unprepared.

The guide included "The 10 Principles of Burning Man," a counterculture manifesto and was based on the ethic of maximum personal freedom in balance with maximum personal responsibility. Radical self-expression was encouraged in a context of community collaboration, untainted by commercial exploitation. A gift economy prevailed. Anyone could be a part of Burning Man. Anyone could bring art to the playa. Anyone could belong. Even me.

Chapter 19

EIGHT MONTHS LATER, I WOULD FIND myself back on the playa. This time it was absolutely quiet—and empty. I felt like Dorothy after she clicked her ruby-red slippers three times. The Emerald City had disappeared. Where were the art cars that glided across the desert floor, mutant vehicles looking like enormous mythical creatures? Where were all the people who had lived here for one glorious week, dressed in fantastic costumes or in various states of blissful nakedness? Where were the "Burners," going nowhere in particular on bicycles, riding across a desert like corrugated cardboard? Where was the music, the heat, the sacred insanity? The silence all around me was like a rest in a musical score. The vastness was palpable. I felt a Gestalt shift in my perception, as if what defined me was the emptiness, not the physicality of my own body.

It was April 2008. I had come with my partner, George, for a long weekend, wanting to experience this dry, alkali lakebed the way the Paiute people had three thousand years before. I half expected to find artifacts from the tribe of Burning Man, a civilization that had been so vibrant just a short time ago. But there was nothing, no trace of Burning Man 2007. As it should be. We "leave no trace," not a forgotten tent stake, no empty plastic water bottles, no piles of ash or bits of burnt wood. Like other desert nomads, we had rolled up our tents and stolen away.

George and I arrived the day before, late in the afternoon, just as the sun began to take cover behind the ragged peaks of Black Rock Mountain. Traffic was sparse on the two-lane road from Fernley to Gerlach, the final outpost, with a population of 206 people.

Tired after a five-and-a-half-hour drive, we needed to find our campsite and get set up before nightfall. Driving slowly onto the playa in my partner's vintage Ford Escort, we surveyed the possibilities. They were endless. One thousand square miles of flat alkali desert and no one here but us. How does one choose a particular location when there are no trees, no rock outcroppings, no protected coves to nestle in? We parked about the length of a football field out on the playa and got out of the car. Stretching my legs after the long drive, I opened the trunk and started hauling out camping stuff. The wind picked up so quickly that we were caught off guard. We tried to lay the tent out, but wind that moments before had seemed like a gentle breeze had gained momentum, lifting up the corners before we could pound in stakes.

George moved the car to act as a windbreak, and I placed a tarp, with the folded-up tent on top, close to the side of the car. We furiously hammered tent stakes into all four corners and hooked two slender poles to the fabric, forming an X. We tried raising the tent, as alkali dust whipped against our faces. Even with a windbreak, the gusts were so strong they almost laid the tent flat, so we jerry-rigged one rope from the top of the tent to the car's rearview mirror and another to a short wooden pole we found in the trunk, tied to the rear bumper. The whole thing looked ridiculous, but at least we had a place to sleep. Cooking was impossible. We ate cheese and crackers for dinner and stuffed ourselves into sleeping bags. George looked at me and said, "So why did we come here?" I didn't answer. He was still in Kansas, knowing nothing about the Emerald City.

After a turbulent night of wind-tossed sleep, interspersed with weird dreams, none of which I remembered, I woke up to absolute stillness. No wind. No sounds at all except George snoring. I wiggled out of my sleeping bag and out of the tent into a glorious, clear, blue-sky morning, fully dressed. I'd slept in my clothes. The playa was a chalk-white floor, covered in hexagonal tiles, still warm under my bare feet. I raised my arms to the heavens and shouted, "Good morning! It's going to be a good day!"

I don't camp without a cone and filter that fits over our plastic mugs. I had just lifted the enamel pot and started pouring boiling water over fine-ground coffee when George emerged from the tent, looking disheveled, rubbing sleep from his eyes. "Coffee smells good. What's next?"

"Let's hike across the playa. The weather's perfect. It'll just take me fifteen minutes to pack a lunch. It's so beautiful." My throat tightened around those last words, and I could feel tears well up. *It's so beautiful.* I felt I had come home.

George said, "You got it," and disappeared into the tent. I could hear him straightening things up. I spread almond butter and honey on wheat bread, slapped sandwiches together, slid them into baggies, and stowed them in my day pack along with a couple of apples. George came out, filled a water bottle for each of us, and we were ready to go.

There was no trail, just an expansive sense of freedom to follow a trajectory more familiar to birds than to land dwellers. A part of me was looking down at the two humans walking purposefully across the vastness of the desert. I lost track of time, just putting one foot in front of the other in that walking meditation so familiar to me. The sun was high when we flopped down on a bed of scrub grass at the edge of the playa, tired and hungry. After lunch we lay back in the scant shade of a greasewood bush, and I let my mind wander. Far off to the east, I could see billowy white clouds tinged with gray oozing over the mountains. *Hmmm. Looks like rain.* "George," I said, "I think we better get going. We don't want to get stuck on the playa in the rain."

We gathered our stuff together and shouldered our packs. By the time we were a quarter of the way across, the wind seemed to come out of nowhere. What had started as light sprinkles very quickly became fat splats of rain that turned the playa a mottled shade of ochre-tinged gray. Then it began to come in sheets, driven sideways by the wind. It looked as if we were, maybe, halfway across. It was hard to see. We could only trudge on, as the desert surface became a lake of mud a few inches deep, not just ordinary mud, but alkali mud, like a slurry of cement that stuck to the tread of our boots, making it harder and harder to walk. What had taken only an hour to cross took more than twice that to return. When we finally reached our camp, it was awash in mud. We were drenched and covered in mud up to our knees. Luckily, the tent was waterproof enough to be dry inside, but the car was marooned. We could go nowhere until the rain stopped, the sun came out, and the lakebed dried up.

This story does have a happy ending. We pulled off our sodden boots, stripped off our soggy clothes, and took shelter in the tent where dry clothes awaited us, laughing at the absurdity of our situation. What else could we do? We even managed to heat up some ramen for dinner on the single-burner propane stove, with mandarin oranges and granola bars for dessert. We were so exhausted it was easy to go to sleep with the sound of rain, now just a shower, drumming against the skin of our tent.

THE NEXT MORNING, SUN SHONE DOWN like a blessing. The lakebed dried out almost as fast as it had become flooded. By afternoon, the hexagonal pattern covered the desert, as if laid by master tile setters. We found two worn one-by-four planks in the brush near our campsite and used them to provide enough traction for the rear tires, so we could back our stuck car out of the mud. We drove home a day early, having had enough adventure for one weekend.

On the long drive back to Calaveras County, deep in thought, I realized that being in the desert in those moments of solitude, I had come home to myself in ways I did not fully understand. I needed this space and time to feel where I might fit into Burning Man 2008, just four months away. I knew I had to return.

Chapter 20

BURNING MAN 2007 WAS MY FIRST TIME. I felt like an unlikely "virgin" being initiated into a tribal ritual old as humankind and contemporary as the electronic music that throbbed all day and all night. Black Rock City had opened its arms wide to me for one glorious week. The playa was a vast surrealist painting by Salvador Dalí, where figures floated above ground like a hallucination and the art itself was larger than life. When George and I left the Black Rock Desert in the spring, I began to imagine the installation I would bring in August.

As soon as I got home and started work on the design, I realized that the seed of the idea had come to me during the mythic sandstorm. Flat on my belly on the earth, practically naked, my body scoured by the wind, I had felt strangely at home in the universe, a creature among creatures. I was inspired by a prayer of the Lakota people, *"Mitákuye oyásin"* ("All our relations"), which celebrates the web of life connecting all beings on Earth. It is a prayer for peace. The theme for Burning Man 2008 was "American Dream." "Mitákuye oyásin" was my dream.

Two weeks before the event , my installation was done. Five black columns, ten feet tall, stood like sentinels in a circle ten feet across. They were made of hollow cardboard cylinders called Sonotubes. A spirit animal, with body and masked face, spiraled around each column to represent the realms of reptile, mammal, insect, bird, and fish. My subjects came from myths about the reciprocal relationship between humans and animals. In Australia, the lizard, Tarrotarro, divided people into male and female and taught them the arts. The Kwakiutl of British Columbia believed that when the ancestors took off their wolf masks, they became humans. In South Africa, the praying mantis was said to have brought the first fire to the San Bushmen, one of the oldest people on Earth. Hawk had the power of prophecy in Polynesian mythology. From Irish folklore, a Salmon of Knowledge, when caught and eaten, gave second sight.

I constructed a pentagram from slender lengths of angle iron and secured each of the five points to the top of a column. At the center, I hung a mobile of the human family. Grandmother, mother and father, and youth and child represented three generations across cultures. Their faces looked toward the world with open eyes. Inside each mask, I sculpted a face of the dreamer with eyes closed. I wondered what they might be dreaming and what dreams would shape our future. Would our dreams sustain life or destroy it for all our relations?

I would be going to Burning Man alone. My buddies from the previous year had a conflicting gig, and Burning Man was the last place George wanted to be after the rainstorm we had experienced. I'd put the word out that I was looking for someone to go with me, there were no takers. But the pull to be there with my art was so strong that it outweighed the voice of reason that said, *What the fuck are you doing going alone?*

The day before my departure, I packed my truck, an old white four-wheel-drive Chevy with a leaky camper shell. I wrapped the masks and animal bodies in bubble wrap, put them in cardboard file boxes, and stowed them inside the camper. The Sonotubes were light enough to be stacked on top of the camper, three on the bottom and two on top. The angle iron, ladder, pick and shovel, and a post-hole digger fit along each side. George helped me tie everything down with bungee cords and rope. An air mattress, sleeping bag, food for a week, and twelve gallons of water fit near the tailgate. My clothes, safety glasses, and a package of dust masks were in my backpack. This time I was prepared. I slammed the tailgate shut and tied my bike on the back. I was ready to go.

I had everything I needed except someone to help set up. I didn't have the strength to dig five two-foot-deep holes in the ground. That night, I got a call from Catherine. "Hey, Sharon. I've got good news. Alan Willard needs a ride to Burning Man. A friend of mine couldn't go at the last minute and gave him a ticket. Can he hitch a ride?"

We had only met once, but I said, "Yes! That's great! Have him call me." Alan Willard and I became friends, swapping stories on the long ride from Calaveras County across the Carson Pass into Nevada, following the pilgrim's trail to Black Rock City.

Because I was bringing art, we were permitted to arrive before the official opening and avoided getting stuck in the excruciating, infamous Burning Man traffic jam. Searching for a place to camp, we drove back and forth on curved streets checking out neighborhoods until we found one that looked promising. It was a cluster of shade canopies and dome-shaped tents in nylon shades of green and blue that looked like mushrooms that had popped out of the soil after a rain. Among the mushrooms were foldout tables, camp chairs, and a funky overstuffed couch. There were mostly men in the camp, maybe six or eight. One man, who was wearing a housedress, waved as we pulled off the road and came over to say hi. He was thirty-something, slender, with short-cropped hair and an easy smile. Alan leaned out of the passenger window to shake his hand, "OK if we stay here?" The man in the dress, a cotton shift with tiny pastel flowers (which looked as if he had borrowed it from his grandmother and actually fit him very well), checked out the load on top of my truck and said, "Yeah. We have plenty of room. I'll show you where you can set up."

That evening, we met our campmates, men with playa names like Bright Eyes, Fringe, and The Wizard. The Wizard was older than me, perhaps in his early seventies, elegant, with a long flowing beard like Gandalf in *The Lord of the Rings*. His beautiful, flamboyant partner, Dark Star, a hair stylist in Beverly Hills, had dyed The Wizard's beard rainbow colors of red, yellow, orange, emerald green, indigo, and purple for the ritual burning of *The Man* on Saturday night. I talked about life, risk-taking, and creativity with the man in the housedress, also an artist, whose wife and kids had stayed at home. He came every year with his cousin, Bright Eyes. This was their break from ordinary life.

On our first night, we were invited to potluck and passed around a gallon jug of red wine. Then Alan and I said good night, leaving me in the back of my truck and Alan in his tent. We had to get up early the next morning to set up my installation.

No motor vehicles are allowed on the playa during Burning Man, except art cars, construction equipment used to install large art pieces, and people driving trucks with their own art on board, like us. We got our assigned location, and followed a guy on an ATV to our site. It was right off the main thoroughfare, maybe 250 yards from *The Man*. I was ecstatic. But we had little time to celebrate, because Alan had five large holes to dig in the hard alkali ground before I could set the Sonotubes, position the heavy angle iron pentagram on top, and secure it in place. Only then could I hang the spirit animals, one on each column, with the family mobile suspended at the center.

By 10 a.m., it was at least ninety degrees. There was no shade. Alan stripped down to naked, a man close to my age with a body strong from working at the cement plant and lumber mill when he was young. He had a pot belly, a full gray beard, and a tan that ended where his shirt and trousers would have been. He wore dark glasses to protect his eyes and an old cowboy hat to cover his bald head. Alan Willard was on a mission. He was going to dig those damn holes, no matter what. Even when a ferocious sandstorm began to build, Alan Willard kept on digging. People stopped and stared in mute admiration. With goggles shielding their eyes and colorful handkerchiefs tied in back to cover their noses and mouths, they looked like bandits. "Hey, buddy. Why don't you get one of those tractors from the Artery to dig those holes?"

But Alan did not stop working. He just said, "Nope. I've got to do it myself," and kept on digging. It was epic. He became the playa's John Henry. Nothin' was gonna stop him. Except nightfall. He left to get something to bring back for me to eat, because I had to stay in the camper with the project. After dinner, we anchored the Sonotubes, rolling around on the ground in the wind, with a piece of angle iron inside each one. Alan left for camp, and I stayed on, listening to the wind whistling through cracks in the camper shell for most of the night.

I WOKE UP ABOUT 6 A.M. WITH THE pale sun casting rectangles of light across my rumpled sleeping bag. My mouth felt as if I'd eaten cotton balls and dust for dinner, and everything in the camper was covered in fine alkali powder. I could hear partygoers staggering back to their camps after a night of revelry and the sound of a hundred porta potty doors slamming shut in syncopated rhythm. And there was music, always music, even at this time of the morning. I flipped up the back window, released the tailgate with a thud, crawled out of my truck, and headed toward the nearest row of potties. We could complete the installation today if we had a break in the sandstorms. I was already dressed, having slept in my clothes.

Breakfast was two granola bars and water. I waited for Alan, perched on the tailgate.

He rode up on his bike with a travel mug full of coffee and milk, a gift from one of our campmates. I drank it as we stood in the center of the circle I had laid out in the sand the day before, using five tent stakes as markers. Three holes had already been dug. With the handicap of yesterday's sandstorm, it had taken at least an hour and a half for each one.

As Alan got to work on the last two, I dropped three Sonotubes into their finished holes. They leaned at odd angles because we hadn't yet packed them all around with sand. Attaching the pentagram to each one at the top would stabilize the whole structure. By noon, Alan had dug all of the holes. Every cylinder was anchored in place when we broke for lunch. This was only the first leg of our race against time and weather to complete the installation before dark. We were back in an hour, working together to attach five lengths of angle iron to form a five-pointed star. By late afternoon, all that was left was to hang the art. I climbed up the stepladder to attach each animal, wrapping the painted fabric body in a spiral around a black column and fastening it with a staple gun. The finishing touch was securing every creature's mask in place—first lizard, then wolf, praying mantis, hawk, and salmon. At the center, I hung the human mobile, each family member suspended from a length of strong fishing line, balancing on two slender, horizontal wooden dowels, grandmother at the bottom, mother and father in the middle, child and youth at the top, in a generational hierarchy. My dream had become a reality.

The sun was setting when Alan and I stood back to admire our work. It was a magnificent desert Parthenon. Black columns in a circle cast long shadows across the sand. The creatures came to life as waning light saturated their colors and brought their mask faces into sharp relief. They had their place, and I belonged here too. Throughout the day, the playa had filled up with Burners on bikes, walking or driving art cars that spun and bounced or glided across the landscape, like psychedelic beetles, armored spiders, spaceships, or a Victorian house. A red leather couch cruised by with a couple comfortably seated as if they were relaxing in their living room. It was followed by a yacht on wheels the size of a bus. People stopped, captivated by the animals spiraling around the columns, encircling a mobile of human masks. They asked, "What is this? Is that really a praying mantis? What's their story?" People, regardless of age, wanted to know the stories. A woman about five feet tall with neon pink hair and butterfly wings jumped off her bike and gushed, "I *looove* the animals, but why people masks?" Two guys dressed in matching S&M leather and chains overheard us talking and joined in an animated discussion about the web of life. It was a perfect ending to a perfect day.

THE BURNING MAN EVENT WAS seven days, ending on Labor Day. There's something biblical about that. Seven is the number of completion. "God created the Earth and everything in it" in seven days. Although it was only day two, I felt more alive, accretions of the last year sanded away by playa dust until there was nothing left but me and the desert, the sun, and the wind. My morning routine started on day three and became a kind of ritual. I woke up with the sun, crawled out of my sleeping bag, and padded in bare feet to the closest porta potty to pee. I dug something out of my box of provisions for breakfast, jumped on my bike wearing jeans and a T-shirt with no bra, and pedaled to a camp serving hot Starbucks French Roast to anyone who needed a caffeine wake-up. Then I rode out to check on *All Our Relations*.

Each morning they greeted me, my five familiars, and the human family that felt like my own. Except on the fourth day. I immediately knew something was wrong. I circled around the columns, greeting each creature, then turned to the mobile in the center. Grandmother was there, as were the two children. But the mother was hanging off-kilter at the end of one of the dowels, and the father was missing. How could this be? I scoured the ground, going around and around in widening circles, thinking that maybe it had been caught by the wind and blown away. No luck. I returned and sat cross-legged between the hawk and the salmon, just looking at the space where the father had been, trying to figure it out. Had someone stolen it? Some drunk twenty-something trying to impress his drunk friends? I was halfway into the story before I stopped. What mattered was the reality that the father was gone. *The father was gone.* I was shaking and sobbing before I knew what was happening. *My father was gone. He had always been gone.*

I flashed back to my old house: I'm seventeen years old, just before I leave home. My parents are getting a divorce and my dad has moved out. My mother, brother, and I are watching television in my brother's bedroom, sitting together on his single bed. *Ozzie and Harriet* is on and the father has just walked in the door, home from work. His wife and kids run to him with smiles and hugs. That was never our family, so why are the three of us crying and hugging? It's the only time we ever cried together, the only time I will ever remember crying over my lost father, other than when he married his mistress after the divorce was final.

Out on the playa, I allowed myself to grieve. The father was gone, and there was nothing I could do about it. Not then. Not now. I thought about clients I had worked with who lost fathers to addiction, divorce, abuse, neglect, and death. I thought about men who were present for their families, my son and my daughter's husband, a couple of uncles, male friends. Then I remembered the men in my camp. I could ask them to let me make masks of their faces to become the missing part of my installation.

When I got back to camp, all the guys were there, just hanging out. It was too hot to do anything else. I told them what had happened and asked for their help. Without exception, they said yes. I commandeered an aluminum chaise lounge and set up what I needed on a camp table: a bowl of warm water, strips of plaster gauze, and a jar of Vaseline. One by one, each man lay back in the chaise lounge and closed his eyes. I covered their faces with Vaseline and tenderly smoothed on wet plaster gauze, appreciating the intimacy of this ritual. The plaster gauze dried quickly. When I finished, six white masks lay in a row on the table, looking back at me. Early the next morning, I hung them in the space where the father had been.

Chapter 21

FROM MY INITIATION AT BURNING MAN in 2007 to my last year in 2011, the community that formed on the Black Rock Desert at the end of August became my tribe. Each time, I felt like I was coming home. Each time I brought my art to Burning Man, I was welcomed.

For five years, one week out of every year, I was exquisitely conscious of living life in the only way possible, moment by moment. All the chaos, the mind-numbing minutiae that occupied too many of my days the rest of the year, was reduced to the four basic elements: earth, air, fire, and water. Alkali dust invaded every orifice. The wind moved sand around in waves and funnels. Only occasional clouds, infrequent rain, and nightfall could interrupt the intense, white-hot sun. And without water, we would perish, or we'd have to drive ten miles to Gerlach, the nearest outpost of civilization.

The spirit of Burning Man was a raucous, holy presence, as simple as someone offering you a cool drink, a frozen Otter Pop, or a shot of tequila, as simple as people telling their stories. Chris was a pipe fitter from Arkansas who read Nietzsche and submitted articles to *The New Yorker*, in spite of repeated rejections. One time, our campmates were two guys and a girl from Israel who had just gotten out of the Israeli army. This was their first experience at Burning Man. The woman's name was Sophia. She'd been a guide before her military service, taking young American Jews on tours of their Promised Land. One evening, we sat together on a quilt spread out between our tents and shared a feast of nachos I'd made using leftover tortilla chips, cheddar cheese shredded with my pocket knife, and a can of black beans heated on my single-burner stove. The Israelis brought tins of sardines, crackers, cold beer, and warm red wine. Sophia spoke of her sadness growing up in Israel, always feeling threatened. Her voice was wistful when she said, "Americans here at Burning Man are so lighthearted."

For one week, we came from all over the world. It was free and generous and wild and crazy and beautiful. We were family. How could I not go back year after year? How could I not bring my art to Burning Man?

For 2009, the theme was "Endangered Species." I was thrilled because I could take the previous installation to another level. Our site was so near *The Man* that it felt as if we were on the same plot of land as the year before. I arranged the six columns in an S curve, the way a snake moves across the desert. On five of the columns were endangered or threatened species: blue-tailed skink, Snake River sockeye salmon, Swainson's hawk, gray wolf, and the Kaua'i cave wolf spider. The sixth column was empty, waiting for life masks of the human species. Why include human beings as endangered? Throughout human history, genocide has eliminated whole communities of people, and it may be too late to reverse climate change, making most living creatures on Earth, including humans, extinct.

As people wove in and out of the columns, I invited each one to sit with me to make a plaster-gauze life mask of their face, to become part of the installation. By Saturday night, when *The Man* burned, the sixth column was filled with stark-white masks against a black background, the faces of my tribe at Burning Man.

My art was evolving, outgrowing the space in my mind that had given birth to the first two installations. It was as if the playa itself had expanded my sense of space. Even the twelve-foot-high Sonotubes were not big enough.

For Burning Man 2010, I envisioned a labyrinth to draw people in and make them part of the art. Wondering what to place at the center, I discovered a female dragon from Lakota Sioux mythology, Uncegila, while reading Brooke Medicine Eagle's book *Buffalo Woman Comes Singing*. She was described as fierce and protective, so who better to watch over Black Rock City? I constructed her out of enormous Sonotube cylinders, cut, shaped, and assembled into a massive environmental sculpture. She was twenty-two feet high and four-feet wide at the base, and she reigned over a classic labyrinth, thirty-two feet in diameter. Shining green scales covered her body, slender neck, and elegant head. Brilliant blue fins ran down her back. On her chest were horizontal bands of armor in the same color as her long claws, orange and gold. She sat on her haunches with front legs and body open to welcome those who walked the labyrinth to her center. At night, solar lights illuminated Uncegila. Burners came at all times of the day and night, laughing, talking, or sometimes quietly tripping down the labyrinthine path. It was magical. It was Burning Man. There was nowhere else on Earth like it.

THE THEME FOR BURNING MAN was always announced in January. Right after New Year's, I checked the website daily. After the labyrinth, a new idea had been growing in my mind for 2011. Although artists brought whatever they wanted, I enjoyed the synchronicities that often arose between the chosen theme and what I had been imagining for my installation. When "Initiation" was posted, I was ecstatic.

I had been reading *Of Water and the Spirit*, a memoir by Malidoma Somé, a member of the Dagara tribe in Burkina

Faso in West Africa. As a young boy, he was very close to his grandfather, a tribal elder and shaman. Malidoma was only four years old when his grandfather died, and his parents, converts to Christianity, sent their son away to be educated by the Jesuits. His education included physical and emotional abuse. He escaped when he was twenty and found his way back to his people, but he did not feel a part of the Dagara community or of the Western world. The elders met in council and decided that Malidoma needed to be initiated in the Dagara tradition. Only then could he move forward as a man and know his purpose in life. Initiation happened in three stages: separation, ordeal, and homecoming. Malidoma survived the ordeal and completed his initiation, but where would his place in the world be?

The Dagara believe that when someone has harmed another person, both people need healing, but the one who has done harm may be the most in need. The elders were very aware of the power of the West and the abuse of that power. Because of Malidoma's formative experience with the Jesuits, they determined that his purpose in life would be to teach the Dagara ethical belief system and practice of initiation in the West. To complete his education, Malidoma was sent to the Sorbonne in Paris, and then to the United States, earning three master's degrees and two doctorates. He teaches at Brandeis University and leads workshops in the United States and Europe.

Initiation as a process of change includes separation from the familiar, the chaotic experience of an ordeal, and coming home. Learning this was transformative for me. It provided a different way of understanding what was missing in our fast-paced, success-driven age, where initiation rituals, independent of religious dogma, were absent.

I started with drawings, played with images of the three stages, and imagined them swirling around a cylindrical core. I wanted to release the spiral in the Sonotube. Any tube you use is a flat sheet of cardboard cut diagonally and rolled into a cylinder. Check out the one in a roll of toilet paper. Sonotubes are exactly the same, only much bigger. What emerged from my experimentation were three sculptures: *Separation*, the dolphin, a mammal who lives in the water and breathes air but cannot return to land; *Ordeal*, a Phoenix rising from the ashes of the alkali desert; and *Homecoming*, three "Dust Dancers," similar to dust devils, circling around each other in a dervish dance of welcome. Each figure was four feet in diameter and, like the dragon, the center of a classic labyrinth. They ranged in height from sixteen to twenty feet. The first labyrinth flowed into the second and the second flowed into the third, to replicate the dynamic relationship that connected each of the three stages of *Initiation*.

What excites me most about the creative process is the resonance between life and art when the energy of a project oscillates with life, expanding and deepening the meaning of the work. In hindsight, I realized that I had naively chosen this subject without factoring in the cataclysmic nature of unintended consequences. But how could I have foreseen that this year would be marked by ordeal? How does one prepare for the unknown, for a dark night of the soul? How could I have known that this year would be my last Burning Man?

It took nine months to complete this complex environmental sculpture. Not having an excavator or a crane, I designed the sculptures in sections so they could be transported and assembled at Burning Man, using their equipment and operators to dig three big holes in the hard-packed earth and to erect the massive figures. When I packed up and left for Burning Man, I didn't know if the engineering would work. I didn't know if my art would actually come to life on the playa.

The three sculptures were so big it required a community to install them. My crew was my partner, George, my grandson Cory, his cousin Curt, a Burner named Rebar, and my eighty-seven-year-old mother, who wanted to know firsthand what I had been doing every summer for the last five years. Working together, it took a day and a half to unload all the parts and assemble them on-site in ninety-degree heat. Thank God there were no sandstorms. When we were done, the Dolphin, Phoenix, and Dust Dancers lay as if asleep, waiting for the magic that would resurrect them. The Phoenix, twenty feet high, with flaming wings that spanned fifteen feet, was the most challenging. A crane operator lifted it up from the desert floor, suspended from what looked like a fragile, steel umbilical cord. It swayed back and forth as he slowly positioned it above a hole that seemed hardly big enough and gently dropped it in place. I held my breath. Would it stand, or collapse under its own weight? It held.

I shouted, "We did it!" I felt like a mother who had just given birth to a very big baby, and that my crew, a bunch of guys whom I loved, were the midwives.

That week at Burning Man, I lived a magnificent lifetime—and then it was done. On Saturday night, *The Man* burned. Fifty thousand people and hundreds of art cars swarmed out onto the playa in an improvisational procession, circling around the monumental sculpture. At its apex, the iconic image waited. Fireworks blotted out the stars, spinning like Van Gogh's *Starry Night*. The excitement built until the intensity was so great you could feel it vibrating in the air. In front of the Phoenix, a lone woman danced in gauzy harem pants, swirling a flame-tipped baton in each hand. The fire began at the base of *The Man* and burned hot, up and up and up. The crowd roared along with the roar of the flames. Burning Man. It's about fire.

A day and a half after we returned home, a wildfire burned across our land. Smoke clouds, stained red by the flames, billowed up into the afternoon sky, blocking out the sun. Silhouetted against the smoking sky, a lone helicopter carried a small bucket of water to try to extinguish an inferno, while an airplane dove low, spraying orange fire retardant. Off in the distance, the wail of a fire truck sounded like a lament.

Forty of our eighty acres of trees and brush burned to the ground. Our house, and my daughter and son-in-law's, survived. My studio survived. There is a way in which each year, Burning Man is a chosen initiation. I had thought the initiation was over when we came home, but I realized that *Homecoming* isn't an end. It's part of the cycle of life: birth . . . life . . . death . . . birth . . . life . . . death. The winter rains would come. The land would turn green in the spring, but the change was absolute. It would never be the land I left when we went to Burning Man. It would be something new, and something very, very old.

Chapter 22

THE HARDEST INITIATIONS are those we don't choose and the incomplete ones where there is no homecoming.

A day after the fire, we were allowed to return home, after having to evacuate. George and I walked the mile-long trail that encircled our burned forty acres, sidestepping hot spots, where the fire still smoldered. A few firefighters in yellow suits were working to extinguish them. Halfway up the trail, the fire captain stood with his back to us. As we approached, he turned and registered surprise that we were there. "It's not safe for you to be here," he stated flatly.

I looked him full in the eyes and said quietly, "We live here." My voice caught in my throat. "I just wanted to see if anything survived . . . the trees . . ." I couldn't go on.

Holding my eyes with his, he said, "I'm so sorry. Go ahead. Just be careful."

I touched his hand and said, "Thank you. Thank you for saving what you could." The trail, cut by hand over weeks by my friend Keith, was nearly obliterated by gray ash, blackened bits of leaves and branches, and charred tree trunks.

As I grieved, I became obsessed with the archetypes of transformation through fire. I envisioned a sculpture of

Quetzalcoatl, the Aztec feathered serpent, symbol of death and resurrection. It would be my next Burning Man installation, and I planned to burn it ritually on the playa. At its center I would create a steel sculpture of the Staff of Asclepius, a branch encircled by a serpent, the universal symbol of healing. When Quetzalcoatl burned, the staff would survive, left standing in the ashes at its base.

When the theme for 2012, "Fertility," was announced in early January, it did not inspire me, but passion for my subject had already been ignited. I knew how to create very large Sonotube sculptures, but I had not sculpted with metal before. I bought a used MIG welder, found someone to teach me how to use it, and designed a scrap-metal shed to do it in. George and a friend of his built it. At a deeper level, I sensed the undertow of another initiation. It would be about fire and loss and letting go and healing. I felt driven by this fire in my belly.

My first priority was to buy tickets, so I checked my email to see when they would go on sale. I saw the familiar address and clicked on. I couldn't believe what was on the screen. For 2012, event organizers had replaced first-come-first-serve online sales of tickets with a lottery. *Who the hell are the "event organizers," and what are they thinking?* I read the information through three times, feeling incredulous, shocked, and then angry. *What the fuck! I could work for the next nine months and not get in!* I didn't have time to wait for the roll of the lottery dice to start work on my installation. Then the enormity of what had been decided dawned on me. Everyone but the elite in the Burning Man community and lucky lottery winners were going through the same ordeal, people like me who made art for the playa, built art cars, created theme camps, made the music, provided medical care, and acted as peace officers. As a collective, we were the infrastructure of Burning Man. This crisis became national news. The *New York Times's* headline for February 12, 2012, declared in bold letters: "Burning Man Festival Regulars Lose Out on Tickets."

I felt betrayed and disillusioned with the Burning Man establishment. The lottery shut out thousands of people whose commitment was all year long, not just for one week in August. They also raised ticket prices to bring in more income and abandoned their commitment to one of the ten founding principles of Burning Man: "Our community seeks to create social environments that are unmediated by commercial transactions. We stand ready to protect our culture." I actually ordered two tickets and was a lottery "winner," but my trust in the organization's integrity was shattered. I returned the tickets. My installation would exist only in my mind.

FALL OF 2012 WAS COLD AND DRY. The Sierra snowpack, predicted to be 30 percent of normal, was at its lowest since the drought twenty years earlier. The Art Gallery in Murphys had also been experiencing a drought in cash flow since the Great Recession of 2008. George's and my collectors were the middle-income people most affected. When you are facing foreclosure, you don't buy art. When we opened in 2005, there were seven galleries on Main Street. A Saturday Night Art Walk attracted visitors from LA, San Francisco, and Sacramento. Four years later, only two galleries were left.

The financial disaster devastated communities across the nation, and our poor rural county was no exception. With a disproportionate number of low-income families, people were suffering financially, including many of my therapy clients, and some were losing their homes to foreclosure. "Notice of Trustees Sale" announcements in the *Calaveras Enterprise* filled more pages than the rest of the newspaper. Some landlords exploited the crisis, raising rents as available properties disappeared. I was struggling to make the lease payment on the gallery with no income from art sales, and I continued to make masks, wondering when the source of their inspiration would come to an end. I felt like an aging Vestal Virgin, trying to fan the creative flame that had once burned with such intensity.

Calaveras County is like a very small town. Everybody knows everybody else, or someone who does. People knew me either as artist Sharon Strong or Dr. Armstrong, the psychologist. Not only was the public invited to gallery events, but I presented mask-making workshops as an artist/psychologist to the entire sixth grade at the local middle school, teens on probation and their probation officers, as well as weekend classes at the gallery. It was also not uncommon to run into a client at Sender's Market or Kelly's Drugs who would see me and say, "Hi, Dr. Armstrong. How're you doin'?" I had to be careful not to ask, "And how are you?" because they would sometimes tell me in great detail.

One of my favorite encounters happened at the end of a session with a woman about my age who had been my client for several months. As she stood up to leave, she asked, "Is it OK with you if we go out through the gallery? I've never seen your art." I thought for a moment and said yes. She began to look at the masks, one by one, without saying a word. Then she stopped dead still before the dark face of Kali. A skull dangled from her blood-red tongue. Unable to take her eyes off the Hindu goddess of destruction and protection, she said, "No wonder you understand me."

On one blustery October afternoon, a Vietnam vet came in for his appointment carrying a cardboard box about the size of a shoebox. He held it out to me. "I want you to have this. I know you sometimes make masks with snake skins. It's a shed skin. Burmese python. Sixteen feet long."

I took it from him, holding it in both hands as if it might break if I dropped it, feeling overwhelmed by his gift. I had never seen a sixteen-foot snake, let alone a shed skin this size.

It took a few moments before I could say, "Thank you. I will treasure this. Where did it come from?"

He told me the python had been his pet and lived in the basement until it outgrew its terrarium. Then he gave it to a zoo. "That was a while ago. Last time he shed, I just rolled it up into this box and put it on a shelf. You know that Medusa mask you made, with snakeskins for hair? Well, that's what gave me the idea."

That evening after work, I went into my studio and placed the box in the center of my worktable as if it held a ritual object. I had no idea what to do with it. Then, one morning, I opened the door to the studio and knew. Circling the table like a cat closing in on its prey, I drew the box to me, carefully removed the tape that held it closed, and opened the lid. It seemed strange to find the skin there, coiled around itself. I swept the studio and cleared a space big enough to unroll it. When I lifted the Burmese python skin out of the box, it unfurled in my arms. I knelt on the floor and spread it out. It was magnificent. On its back, the shed skin felt like delicate Japanese rice paper. It rippled in a pattern of small hexagonal shapes in shades of raw umber, with a darker area down the center that resembled hearts, broken unevenly. When I turned it over to look at the belly, I caught my breath. Unlike rice paper, each translucent scale was thick as a fingernail, two inches long. Although the same hexagonal pattern was repeated, the shapes were larger, with sharp corners and elongated sides, looking like miniature leaded-glass windows in a Victorian house. I sat back on my heels. The words *End of Time* sounded in my mind as if I had spoken them aloud. Then an image came of an elder with a face so ancient it looked as if it was dissolving into the skull. Its skeletal arms were raised, bent at the elbows, with hands cupped as if holding an offering. The elder was wearing a simple kimono made from the shed skin of the Burmese python.

I had never experienced a work of art emerge so completely and suddenly in my consciousness. I knew exactly what to do, without preliminary sketches, without research, without fear. I sculpted the elder's face over my life mask, the face of an old woman. Shaping clay to bring a mask into being has always been sacred practice for me, ritualistic in an intimate way. I stroked the clay, handling it tenderly, as if making love to a part of myself that had not yet matured. How could I have known so intuitively what she looked like, her nose like mine, her expression defined by the map of lines around eyes and lips and hollow cheeks? I twisted copper wire to form bones for her arms and hands, shaping each finger carefully to capture the gesture of cupped hands. Then I sculpted clay over the bones to create muscle and skin. When the head, neck, and arms had air-dried, I sanded the fine white clay to a satin-smooth finish and brushed on powdered charcoal to accentuate her features. I used a metal coat hanger for shoulders and attached arms to each end and the head to a hook at the top. Then I was ready to create a kimono out of the shed skin.

In many pre-Judeo-Christian cultures, the snake was revered as a symbol of transformation, shedding the old skin to reveal new skin underneath. Because all life is a process of birth, life, death, and transformation, it was deeply meaningful for me to make the elder's robe out of the python's shed skin.

I cleared my worktable to make space. The kimono would be six feet long. I folded the skin in half, cut two feet off the bottom to make sleeves, and cut a slit at the top for the neck opening. I lifted the front of the half-finished garment, passed the head and neck through the opening, and wrapped the sleeves over the arms. Everything fit perfectly. I hand-sewed the sides and attached the sleeves with long strands of white horse hair. A shaman's medicine bag hung on a leather thong around her neck, a tiny hummingbird nest filled with soft feathers and a small bird skull. I closed the neck opening using crossed porcupine quills to form an X. It was complete. I felt a profound sense of fulfillment, as well as the small death that always comes when an important, personal work of art was finished. It was late afternoon. I was tired and feeling melancholy, so I brewed some coffee, poured a cup, and looked down at *End of Time* lying on the table.

Suddenly I felt a sense of urgency to hang it on the north wall of the studio. With growing excitement, I climbed a ladder and hammered three nails into the wall to hold the head and hands. Cradling the shoulders, arms, and head in one arm, being careful not to step on the kimono, I went up the ladder again to hang *End of Time*. When it was done, relief overwhelmed me, and I sank into a nearby chair.

The shed snakeskin embodied transformation, the sloughing off of what was dead, so that what was alive could emerge. But the name, *End of Time*, seemed antithetical to the process of transformation. *What is alive and what is dying?* ran through my mind like a koan. My feeling of melancholy deepened as I thought about this. It wasn't just depression about the financial disaster of the last four years, as destructive as that continued to be. It was deeper and darker. Climate change came to mind, and the term *global warming*.

I had struggled for three decades to find words, metaphors, stories for something so all-encompassing and terminal, so massive and devastating that I couldn't get my mind around it. I read. I researched. I shut the feelings off. I felt numb, terrified, impotent. Most of all, I grieved the unimaginable. But how does one grieve what cannot be imagined, except in horrific bits, like pictures flashed on the screen of a nightmare? How does anyone grieve the slow, inexorable death of life on Earth? I don't think we have words to encompass it. Climate *change*? Global *warming*? One sounds like variations in weather between winter and spring and the other like a setting on the microwave. We don't even have rituals to bring us together in grief. A global ecological funeral? A memorial service for the earth while there are still humans to grieve?

Melancholy morphed into a cold hopelessness in the pit of my stomach. My mind spun webs of thoughts with no recognizable pattern until I had to stop. At that exact moment, a gust of wind blew in through an open window, caught the edge of the kimono, and lifted it into the air, shifting the body so that it looked as if it were dancing. I watched transfixed. When it stopped, the gesture of the figure had changed. It no longer looked still and somber. It looked alive. I thought about the ritual for the dead called a *celebration of life*, when the final words in the performance piece I created after my dad died, *Dancing on My Father's Grave*, came to mind:

I am alive and I can see a phoenix rising from the ashes.

Perhaps this work of art was my phoenix rising, my celebration of life, my hope in the face of hopelessness, manifesting what could not be put into words. I was not naive. I was scared. I was committed to do whatever I could as an elder woman, as part of the human family, to heal the planet. And I was alive.

Chapter 23

CHRISTMAS 2012 CAME TO THE TOWN of Murphys on the first Friday in December with a parade, as it had for the seven years we had been on Main Street. I knew it would be our last.

The *End of Time* was displayed in the gallery as I had visualized it, hanging on a black panel suspended from the beams of a ceiling fourteen feet high. On this festive evening, the heavy iron doors of our historic building were flung open, and I could hear the local high school band playing Christmas carols as they marched by. I was upstairs in the loft, putting finishing touches on a tray of hors d'oeuvres and tending a Crockpot full of hot mulled wine, when I stopped to admire the scene below. The gallery was decorated with gold and silver ornaments and the green leaves and red berries of the toyon that grew on our land, tied with gold ribbon. The walls were alive with George's and my art, landscapes that captured the beauty of the Sierra foothills, this county and its historic towns, and my art masks, seeming so present and sentient, waiting like me for the throng of people who would come in after the parade, filled with holiday spirit.

That winter was a strange one, with unusually mild weather. The Bear Valley ski resort, an hour's drive up Highway 4 from

Murphys, didn't get snowfall until just before Christmas. The New Year of 2013 was so quiet, it seemed as if February had snuck in under the radar. On the afternoon of Tuesday, February 19, when I opened the office door to say goodbye to my two o'clock client, we were startled to see the sky filled with dark gray clouds and snow falling so heavily it obscured the walkway. During the session, we'd heard a light rain beginning to fall on the metal roof, and then silence, as rain turned into soft snowflakes. Because it rarely snowed at this elevation, I was surprised it had come on so fast. But my next client was already waiting, so I thought, *No problem. I'll just call to cancel my last appointment and head home as soon as I'm done.*

At four o'clock, when I locked up and hurried to my car, an ominous twilight had enveloped the land. Snow covered everything, roofs and sidewalks, parked cars, and the road I needed to take to get home. I felt apprehensive. There were no chains in my trunk. I had to get home safely as fast as I could, and I began to worry in earnest, thinking, *Oh my God. Once I turn off the paved road, how am I going to make it up the dirt road to my house?* I could park at the bottom of the hill and walk. But in these shoes? I might as well go barefoot. This wasn't good. Then I told myself to just shut the fuck up and drive.

Murphys Grade Road is downhill and winding. I'd driven it hundreds of times, but not like this. There was no one on the road but me. It was already icy. I slowed to ten miles per hour so I wouldn't spin out on the curves. All I could see in the headlights was a blizzard, but I couldn't stop. By the time I hit Highway 49 and turned right, there was a line of commuters in both directions, barely moving. I thought, *There's no way I'm going to get home*, and I began to look for the Travelodge, a quarter mile up the road. There was only one other car in the parking lot. Every building on either side of the road was dark. The only illumination came from the line of cars stuck in traffic on the highway, white headlights pointing north and red taillights pointing south.

I parked and slogged through the snow to the office. An Open sign was on the door. Behind the desk, a young woman holding a flashlight checked me in. It was lucky I had cash to pay for my room, because there was no electricity. Why did they have no backup generator? She handed me a key, a flashlight, and extra blankets. It was going to be a long night, but I was just grateful to have shelter.

In the morning, the sun was shining, and the main roads were clear. On my way to work, wearing the clothes I had worn the day before, I stopped at Save Mart to get something for breakfast, a toothbrush, toothpaste, and makeup. A headline in the *Calaveras Enterprise* read "Snowstorm Wreaks Havoc Across Motherlode." Schools had closed, a thousand households had lost electricity, and a thirty-car pileup closed Highway 4 between Murphys and Bear Valley. Thank God there were no fatalities.

The freak storm in our small part of the world seemed insignificant in the face of hurricanes with names like Katrina, Isaac, and Harvey, tornados in the Midwest, flash floods on the Gulf Coast, and a wildfire season in the Western United States that was increasing with each year as average temperatures reached record highs. But the intensity of our snowstorm seemed to portend climate change in a very local, personal way, maybe because it came so unexpectedly and there was no way I could prepare for it. I struggled with a pervasive sense of dread, and there were days when I seemed to be losing the battle against hopelessness. Although life went on as normal, nothing seemed "normal" anymore. A pattern was beginning to emerge, like a fractal, a pattern of endings. Burning Man, my relationship with George, our gallery, my love affair with mask-making—it all seemed to be coming to an end.

The Art Gallery in Murphys closed in early spring. George and I had saved the final day of packing for the art. Our gallery, which had once been so alive, was silent. Paintings and masks hung in somber solitude, waiting to be taken down, packed in bubble-wrap, covered in brown paper, and stored in boxes. We didn't say much as we worked. George wrapped his paintings, and I packed my art masks.

The last piece to be taken down was *End of Time*. I spread a white sheet on the floor and climbed a ladder, just as I had done before. Gently, I removed the head and hands from their nails and cradled the elder's head and outstretched arms in the crook of my arm. The kimono brushed against my jeans as I climbed down, trying not to step on it. I laid the body on the sheet and carefully folded it over until *End of Time* was completely covered, as if in a shroud. I was crying quietly. George was standing nearby. I stood up and turned toward him. We held each other for a long time. I think we both knew that our relationship was over. What had held us together for so many years was the gallery, and now it was gone.

I still had my small barn house on eighty acres and an art studio I built in 2010 just down the road. Although it looked out over a desolate burnscape, it was surrounded by hundreds of acres of Bureau of Land Management land and forty acres that was still green and wild, a home for deer, quail, jackrabbits, rattlesnakes, and the occasional black bear. But without the gallery, there was no venue for my work. I could market to other galleries here and in the Bay Area, but my heart wasn't in it. My heart was broken, and I didn't know how to mend it. I didn't know what to do. I felt as if the muse that had been my familiar since I was a child had abandoned me.

Rage

Grief

Phoenix

Earth

Shekinah

Infinite Wisdom

Eve

Uncegila, Dragon Labyrinth

End of Time

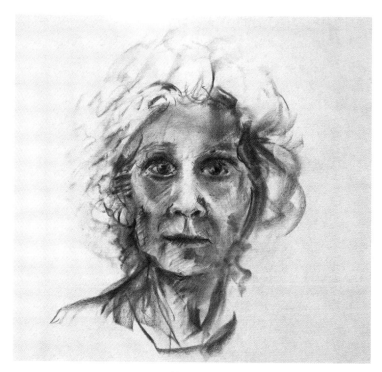

Self-Portrait

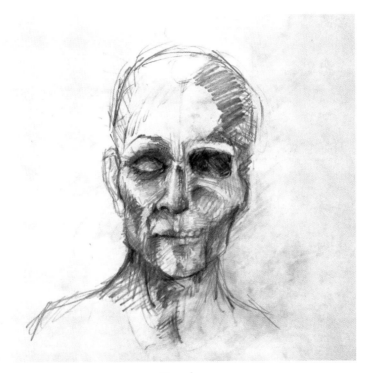

Death

Sewer

Floating

Naked

The Sacred Crack

To Know the Dark

Part Two

Chapter 24

IT ALL STARTED WITH A PSYCHIC reading in 2012, the year of too many endings. My disillusionment with Burning Man, the loss of our gallery, and any hope for a deeper relationship with George had left me feeling sad and stuck. I'm a dreamer. I love imagining what could be possible and then making it happen, but when I dipped into my creative well, it was dry. Carolyn, a close friend, suggested I consult her psychic, John Huddleston. What a good idea! Maybe someone with the gift of clairvoyance could see further than I was able to.

John opened our one-hour phone session with a statement that my life was indeed in turmoil. However, I had the resources, personally and professionally, to overcome the obstacles to leading a fulfilling life. That seemed like a pretty generic beginning for a psychic reading, and I began to wonder why I had done this. Then John zeroed in on my hunger for community and for an intimate connection with a man who got me, who knew me so well he could finish my sentences. He said George was incapable of this and had gone as far as he could. He didn't have "a fire in his belly," and I was seeking that for myself and in a lover. I thought, *Yeah, that's real.*

Then he told me that I was aging backward, and there was a man I hadn't met yet, younger than me, who would "feed my soul." It would be the first equal relationship I would have, and it would change both of our worlds. He even embellished this by adding that we would have two homes, and his would be home base. That was when he began to lose me. I was already in a relationship that was dying a slow death. I didn't need to hear that I would meet an attractive stranger who would change my life. It was such a cliché. I was already overwhelmed with trying to make my own changes. Two years later, Tom Weidlinger walked into my life.

IT WAS NEARING CHRISTMASTIME AGAIN. I needed a break from work, from the confines of my small home and small county. I went to spend the weekend with Carolyn in Berkeley. Her husband of fifty years had died just a few weeks before, and she was grieving. All of us who loved Carolyn and Herb were grieving. The only comfort I could offer was being with her. It was where I needed to be that weekend. We cooked together, danced in her studio, and talked into the night.

Carolyn got Sunday matinee tickets to "The Holiday Revels," a cultural event that was ecumenical in the broadest sense. Over breakfast, she mentioned her friend Tom, a documentary filmmaker, who was alone for the holidays. She suggested we invite him to join us. Tacked to her dining room wall, covered with photos of family and friends, was a snapshot I loved of Carolyn and Tom sailing in San Francisco Bay, with Tom at the helm. I said yes, I wanted to meet him, particularly after Carolyn showed me his film, *Heart of the Congo*. I was interested in his story of aid workers in a rural village helping to save refugee children dying of malnutrition during the civil war. Tom had a way of seeing all the people in his film with compassion, up close. They seemed comfortable being open with him.

We had just finished lunch when a knock on the door announced Tom's arrival. Carolyn rose to answer. Tom was taller than I'd imagined, six foot six. They hugged and she introduced us, asking him to join us for coffee. We sat at Carolyn's round oak table. Tom was to my left. He took a sip of coffee and leaned toward me, his gray-blue eyes looking frankly into mine. "Tell me about yourself."

I was immediately intrigued. A man who wanted, first of all, to know about me? How novel. I responded with, "What do you want to know?"

"Carolyn showed me a picture of one of your sculptures. I think it's called *End of Time*. That piece is really intense. It reminded me of old age and death, decrepitude. It's actually kind of ghoulish."

A dialogue was on, a real exchange, not just social chat. I wanted to open up to this man, but I needed to know more about him.

"How did you relate to it?"

"I was drawn to it because it was so unlike . . . it's not ordinary. It's not beautiful as art. It's not pretty, and yet it is compelling. So, what inspired you to make this?"

I looked at him full in the face and liked what I saw: curly, silvery-gray hair that needed a cut, smile lines and wrinkles around deep-set eyes, a strong jaw. "The figure is an elder. Her garment, the shed skin of a Burmese python, is about transformation. It's about birth and life and death. Right now, I'm going through a lot of endings. It was very powerful and intense to create that piece."

Tom looked thoughtful. "From my first impression of the photograph, I didn't know it was a snakeskin, but I felt that there was something there, not just something to frighten children."

I responded, "Or grown men." We both laughed.

"Carolyn told me that you used your face as the base for the mask. You made yourself into this really old person, so you weren't afraid of that. I thought that was beautiful."

I looked across the table at Carolyn, who had been following this exchange with great interest, and smiled. She returned my smile with a nod of her head, and I went on. "This time in my life is really important. Aging. I don't want to miss it. Making *End of Time* was part of that."

Now it was Tom's turn to answer my questions. "I want to know about your film *Heart of the Congo*. What was it like to be there, as a person and not just a filmmaker?"

"It was the hardest film I've ever made," he began slowly, choosing his words. "I was surrounded by death and suffering. There were times when it was scary. I got malaria and could have died. As an American filmmaker, I was one of only a few people who could be medevaced out of the remote outpost of Malemba-Nkulu, three hundred miles from the nearest paved road, where it seemed like everyone else was dying. It was sobering to be confronted with death on so many different levels."

It was quiet in Carolyn's kitchen. Tom continued, looking down at his hands as if they held the story. "Beautiful things happened too. People welcoming me, the willingness of people to work with me. My stepson was my soundman. After I got sick, he took care of me, and two aid workers took up the cameras and continued filming. It was a journey."

Tom looked up and caught my eyes. I said, "Thank you, Tom." I knew then that I wanted to know this man better.

As we got ready to leave for the performance, I ran upstairs to get my jacket. Carolyn told me later that Tom asked her, "Is she free?" Carolyn said to him that she thought I was. I told her, "Yes! Tell him I'm free. I am freer than I've ever been in my life!"

After the performance, Tom drove us home. He got out of the car, gave each of us a hug, and said good night. He added that he had had a good time. Then he turned to me and suggested that I check out his website, to let him know if there were other films I'd like to see. He offered to put DVDs in the mail, and I could return them after the holidays. "Thank you. Yes." My mind was racing. Was this Tom's pickup line? If it was, it worked. I was already thinking about seeing him again.

Christmas isn't my favorite holiday for a lot of reasons, beginning with my first divorce. I was twenty-four; my kids were two and five years old. Their father had them every other weekend, half the summer, half of Christmas, and alternate years for all the other celebrations. Anyone who has gone through this fragmentation of family holiday rituals knows what I'm talking about. It's hard on everybody, but especially the children. Now mine were grown, with children of their own, but the melancholy had always hung around on holidays. I got through Christmas with minimal ceremony and was relieved when New Year's Eve passed without fanfare. I had met Tom only three weeks earlier but had a sense that the New Year might hold something interesting for both of us.

Tom sent three of his documentary films, *Boys Will Be Men*, *Original Minds*, and *Radical Adjustments: The Life and Times of Marilyn Reed Lucia*. They dealt with issues I cared about: growing up male in the United States, kids with learning differences, and what it was like to be a woman who broke the rules, divorcing when "good" women didn't do that, and becoming an MD while raising four children. I watched all three the first week of the New Year. With each film, Tom Weidlinger became even more interesting to me. I emailed him, telling him how beautiful and real his films were, and suggested we meet in Sausalito on January 23 for lunch, my treat. I told him I would be driving from my home in Mountain Ranch to stay with my daughter, Lisa, on her houseboat for the weekend. Tom lived in Berkeley, so it would be convenient for both of us. He said yes.

Lisa had already left for work when Tom arrived. I heard his footsteps on the wooden ramp and felt a delicious anxiety.

I waited a few moments to calm myself, then opened the door. He filled the doorway. I just stood there and took him in before inviting him to come in. "Did you have any trouble finding Main Dock? I just made a latte. Would you like one?" I felt relaxed and nervous at the same time, wondering if it showed. Tom explored the houseboat while I made his latte, and we sat down to talk about our work, our lives, our marriages and divorces. The conversation continued on our walk to Anchorage 5 café, over eggs Benedict and a second latte. I put my arm in Tom's as we walked back to the houseboat and asked, "Would you like to come in?"

"Yes."

Tom settled into an overstuffed chair near the couch where I sat. We were quiet, just looking at each other. Tom asked, "May I sit next to you?"

"Yes."

I could smell his scent and feel the intimacy of his body close to mine.

"May I kiss you?" he asked.

"Yes."

The kiss was like a continuation of our conversation, only soft and probing. I could feel his fingers in my hair, his face in my hand. We drew apart and sat quietly, each in our own thoughts. We were grown-ups, not teenagers. We were mature adults. We talked about the experience we had just shared, how real and deep it was for each of us. We talked about being wise and going slowly. We agreed that we wanted to see each other again and hugged goodbye, but a part of me wanted to lead Tom into the bedroom and have my way with him.

That weekend was the beginning of an emotional roller-coaster ride that started with Tom on the houseboat doorstep and ended with . . . ? I don't think it has ended. Our relationship began with two people who wanted to be real and take risks, to push the envelope that keeps one stuck in a half-life. Our passion to live fully and deeply as individuals in an intimate relationship was there from the beginning.

EMAIL DOESN'T SUPPORT GOING slowly. It's so easy to quickly type words on a screen, hit the send button, and whoosh, the other person receives what you have written instantly. If you have second thoughts, it's too late to delete. That night, Tom wrote to invite my daughter and me to a small dinner party at his house the following evening. He closed with, "I just wanted to say good night and that I am thinking of you. Thank you for a wonderful afternoon. I don't really have the words to express fully how I feel and I'm trying not to rush to conclusions or label what just happened between us. You are a strong, awake, and beautiful woman, and I feel very at ease with you. See you soon."

The next morning, I emailed back, "Your words echo my experience. After you left I went for a walk on the docks feeling deep contentment, and the excitement of meeting someone new who interests me, and to whom I am attracted. What is important to me is exploration, not projection, and allowing time for discovery. Lisa is looking forward to meeting you. See you tonight." I had no second thoughts.

Discovery was happening quickly. Tom wrote after the dinner party, "Good night, Sharon. I send you a kiss."

I woke at 2 a.m., after dreaming of Tom sitting in a chair next to my bed as I fell asleep. This was unusual, since we had just met. The next morning, I ended my email in response to his with, "I return your kiss." We were having sweet foreplay at a safe distance.

Yet we continued to breach the boundary that separated us. It became more permeable with each email exchange and each hour-long phone call at the end of our workdays. The teenager, the grown-up, in Tom and in me, wanted to get together for real, in person. We agreed that I would come to Berkeley in two weeks and stay with Tom for a long weekend.

The next morning, Tom wrote:

I am feeling rather wickedly impetuous. I'm thinking of coming to see you this weekend. What do you say to that? I really am capable of being grown-up and sensible and waiting to see you Friday the 6th. I just want you to know how deeply, how unexpectedly, and how swiftly you are under my skin.
Love, Tom

P.S. If there's not an obvious, practical reason to decline, then a voice inside me counsels, wait 'til morning to decide.

I didn't wait until morning. My response was:

YES and YES and YES.
We seem well matched in our impetuosity. Let's meet halfway. What do you think about a night on a paddle-wheel steamer in Old Town Sacramento?
I love you
Sharon

Tom's response?

YES, YES, AND YES.

How did I know that I loved Tom so quickly, and how could I trust his knowing? It just seemed natural, unforced, unselfconscious. When I said "I love you" to Tom the first time, it was simply putting a name to something that already was. We were not interested in attaching contingencies to the word *love* or fencing it in with expectations. It was our truth in the moment, and living each moment in love with Tom fulfilled me.

I awoke at 1 a.m., pale moonlight streaming in the window of my studio, on the day I was to meet Tom in Sacramento. Private thoughts swirled in my mind, delicious, sexual sensations. *This is the last night I will wonder about what it would be like to make love with Tom. Tomorrow night, I will know. I want to be slow and tender, to savor discovery, to delight in learning our ways of making love for the first time.*

I KNEW TOM HAD ARRIVED AT our hotel, the Delta King, before I did, because I parked my car next to his. The paddle-wheel steamer had carried passengers up and down the river for sixty years between Sacramento and San Francisco. But as I walked up the gangway to meet my lover, I felt as if I was the last passenger to board, and soon we would cast off on a magical journey. Although it was permanently moored, I was right.

Tom met me on the deck just outside the lobby. Forgetting how tall he was, a foot taller than me, I looked up into his face in wonder. This man, this beautiful man, was smiling down at me, his eyes full of love—and longing. I reached up to hug him and felt enveloped by his embrace, comforted and aroused at the same time. Our cabin on the top deck facing the river was almost ready. We sat at a small round table in deck chairs, waiting, hands touching, fingers stroking faces, discovering the shape of an ear, the curve of a neck. Waiting. Finally, the cleaning woman opened the door and smiled at us. Tom held the door for me as I crossed the threshold.

I love the phrase "They shall become one flesh" from the book of Genesis. The dialogue that began in Carolyn's kitchen such a short time ago had deepened to an intimacy not dependent upon words alone. Our joining was absolute, yet allowed space for our individuality. For each of us, it was new to feel such a sense of freedom to explore our sexuality and be so fully who we were with our lover. Driving home the next morning, I felt as if we were two points on a compass, traveling in opposite directions but with the same center.

When Tom got home, he emailed:

I floated back to Berkeley listening to love songs and still feeling your sweet kisses and caresses. I was even singing along with some of those love songs . . . really feeling them. It is a great gift you have given me, and are giving me, and I accept it with deep gratitude and awe. Thank you.
I love you, Tom

I wrote Tom that evening:

Driving back to the foothills, I felt completely peaceful and satiated . . . my body still vibrating from your touch. I felt wave upon wave of subtle body memories, no words, lovemaking that goes on and on, only interrupted by intermittent sleep. And I love you, love you, love you. Thank you for the most passionate twenty-four hours of my life.
Did I say I love you?
Sharon

The next weekend came swiftly. Because I worked Tuesdays, Wednesdays, and Thursdays in my private practice, a "weekend" for me was four days long. On Friday morning, I laid down tracks that I would follow for the next year from my home in Calaveras County to Tom's. Although I passed landmarks familiar to me from ten years of living in Berkeley—Whole Foods on Ashby and Telegraph, the North Berkeley BART

Station, the intersection at Cedar and Sacramento—the route felt different. I was different. I was not the same woman who'd left Berkeley fifteen years earlier. I would be staying with Tom in his home for the first time. We had made love. My longing to be with him again felt overwhelming.

Friends cautioned us about going too fast. On our first date, we had even counseled each other to go slowly, aware of the intensity of our attraction. In our emails, we discussed the need for spaciousness in our relationship and in our individual lives. Were we going too fast? The morning I was to leave for Tom's, I woke up before the alarm, asking myself what going slowly, holding back, would be like for me. There was no hesitation. It would be like diving into a pool halfway. It was too early for either of us to be in balance with the other. My sense was that our relationship would have a dynamic equilibrium, recalibrating as we continued to grow and change. With that insight, I was able to go back to sleep for another hour. When I woke up, I felt at peace.

For the second time, I pulled up in front of Tom's single-story bungalow and turned off the engine. A large magnolia tree shaded the entry, providing a sense of privacy from neighbors on either side. Across the street, a woman working in her garden looked up and waved as I got out of my car and walked to the front door, carrying my overnight bag. I could feel my heart pounding, even as I tried to slow my breathing. I rang the doorbell. Tom answered immediately. We smiled at each other, and Tom drew me into a hug as he closed the door behind us. The quiet and stillness of his house was palpable. A long sofa took up an entire wall to the right of the entry, with an armrest as wide as a footstool. Tom sat down on it, held me close, and said, "I'm so glad you're here."

"Me too."

The living room was open to a dining area that could accommodate eight dinner guests, with a doorway into the kitchen. Through a corner window above the sink, I could see the small garden, an orange tree with fruit just beginning to ripen, and a patio. We walked back through the living room, Tom holding my hand, into the master bedroom with an enormous king-size bed. We laughed about how generous it was compared with the cabin-size one we were last in, looking at each other like conspirators, knowing we would make love in it that night. Then Tom opened a drawer in his chest of drawers and said, "This one is for you." Such a simple gesture. I felt invited into Tom's space, and into his life.

WE WENT TO DINNER THAT NIGHT at Stella Nonna, his favorite Berkeley restaurant. Over dessert and coffee, Tom told me about the book he was writing, and his film, *The Restless Hungarian.*

"My father, Paul Weidlinger, died sixteen years ago. He was brilliant, an architect, and a world-renowned engineer. We weren't close. When I was a teenager, I hated him." Tom was speaking in short sentences, his voice flat, reporting facts to me as if he had said them many times before. Then he stopped and looked at me searchingly, asking a question without saying it out loud. I took his hand. When he started speaking again, his voice was soft. "My mother was diagnosed with schizophrenia before I was born. I was only seventeen when my sister committed suicide."

My eyes filled with tears. All I could say was, "I am so sorry, you were so young."

Tom squeezed my hand gently. "After my father died, my stepmother sent me a large box of his things. It was heavy. I had no idea what was inside. When I cut it open, I found old manila file folders from his desk. I opened one or two but didn't want to go any further. I taped it shut and put it in the back of a closet. I didn't open it again until just a year ago."

I was so engrossed in Tom's story, feeling into his vulner-ability, that I was startled when our server asked, "Is there anything more I can get you?" Tom paid and we walked back to his place hand in hand, our way illuminated by the yellow glow of streetlights. There was a slight breeze and the night air smelled faintly of the ocean. Tom stopped abruptly and turned toward me. "There's so much more I want to tell you," he said, then hesitated. "My father was a good artist. In one of the folders, I found some of his drawings. I'd like you to look at them as a psychologist and tell me what you see. Would you be comfortable doing that?"

It felt intimate for Tom to share his father's drawings with me. I said, "Yes, I would be honored," feeling deeply touched by his request.

The next morning, Tom handed me a worn folder. We were standing in his office. He said, "I'll be in the next room if you need anything," gave me a quick kiss, and closed the door behind him. Part of me felt like an intruder opening a door into another family's attic. I took a deep breath and looked around. The office was large, with good light. A big desk dominated the space. I opened the folder and looked at the drawings. They had been done decades ago in pen and ink, graphite, and soft pastel on fragile sheets of newsprint, and they had the smell of old books.

The psychologist in me was captivated by the symbolic meaning of the images. It was as if Tom's father had responded to a projective test I use with children to understand how they see themselves and their family relationships: Draw a person, family, house, and tree.

I laid the drawings in a semicircle on the hardwood floor so I could get a sense of their stories. Three themes stood out: Paul's sense of himself as a young man making his way in the world; Paul falling in love with Tom's mother, Madeleine; and Paul gradually losing Madeleine after she was diagnosed with paranoid schizophrenia.

One pen-and-ink drawing shows a man with his back to the viewer, towering over a village in the distance. He is naked from the waist up, with broad shoulders and powerful arms. I thought immediately of the philosopher Nietzsche's *Übermensch*. Paul's longing to be a "superman" is palpable, yet he didn't seem that way in most of the other drawings of himself. Madeleine always appears tall, confident, and voluptuous, her gaze direct and sometimes seductive. In Paul's sketches of the couple, Madeleine is very much a woman. Beside her, Paul looks more like an adolescent. The most poignant drawings were done much later, over a period of several years, as Madeleine succumbed to schizophrenia. They are bold chalk portraits of her face, as if Paul is peering into her eyes to see what is going on in her mind. They are stark and disturbing. In the last two, her face is just a mask with sunken eyes.

I felt sadness, as well as tenderness, for Tom's mother and father. Paul's drawings of the three stages of his life were a visual narrative of his coming of age, finding true love, and then losing that love. These stages are also universal. I thought of the love relationships in my life that had ended. I thought of Tom, and this beginning love between us. We weren't young. We didn't have forty years to work through the hard stuff. But we had enough experience to know that "happily ever after" is a myth, and we hadn't lost faith in life and love.

I walked through the house looking for Tom, wanting to talk with him about his father's drawings, about us, about life. I found him in the kitchen making coffee. "Would you like a cup?" he asked.

"Yes. Let's talk. I have so much to share with you."

Chapter 25

OUR NEXT SIX MONTHS HAD ITS own rhythm, like a heartbeat, *thump-thump*, *thump-thump*, with our time divided into two beats. Half of each week I lived in my studio and saw clients at my office in Calaveras County; the other half I lived in Berkeley with Tom. We described this arrangement as our "bifurcated life."

I longed to share my world with Tom, but my small place was barely big enough for me. So why not build a house? Looking for a building site on land that had been untouched by the fire four years earlier, I wandered down a dirt road we called the Bee Box Trail. Years before, my brother kept bees and had bulldozed the road and cleared a pad for his bee boxes. A black bear, coming out of hibernation, had smelled honey and demolished the boxes. They still lay where he had left them.

The view was expansive. To the south, the land sloped into a shallow valley with smooth hills that rose on each side. To the west, five tall gray pines provided shade from the afternoon sun. The pad had been cut in a large, circular shape. I went back to the studio for my long tape to see if it was big enough for a post-and-beam structure. At roughly sixty feet in diameter, it would work.

Inspired by the elegant simplicity of a yurt, I began envisioning a sixteen-sided glass house with a 360-degree view, encircled by a deck. Then Tom and I would each have a home to share, one in the city and one in the country. I drew preliminary sketches while looking for a builder who could literally think outside the box. I found a brilliant green builder who also happened to be a woman. She loved the challenge of my glass house and was willing to do it on a shoestring budget. We were scheduled to start at the end of May.

Tom was enthusiastic about the glass house and the opportunities it would afford for us to be together, in my world as well as his. We talked about Tom renting out his place in Berkeley for six months a year so that we could live together for longer periods of time. As a filmmaker, he had more flexibility in where he could live than I did.

While I was involved with my clinical work, the construction project, and commuting to and from Berkeley, Tom was immersed in *The Restless Hungarian*, his creative child, who lived and breathed at the center of our life. As we grew more deeply in love and into the intimacy of a shared life, we also prepared for a one-month separation. Tom was leaving for Bolivia in August. His parents had emigrated there in 1939. Tom's father was a Hungarian Jew, and Bolivia was one of the few countries that accepted Jews fleeing the Holocaust, especially those with training in architecture and engineering. Tom planned to interview several adult children of the Hungarian émigrés who had worked with his father. There were also archives in La Paz to research, buildings his father had designed to film, and a road trip to an isolated outpost on the border between Bolivia and Chile, the point of entry for all European refugees. I would join him for the month of September.

August was a very long month. It was good to be on my land, watching the bones of my glass house take shape, but I also felt in limbo, somewhere between my old life and my new life with Tom. Parts of me felt spread out along a continuum between then and now. How I could connect all the parts? Would I have to leave some behind?

I loved hanging out with Christa and Bill, my younger daughter and son-in-law, who lived down the road. My land was actually divided into two parcels. When they moved to Calaveras County from Southern California in 2009, I'd deeded forty of my eighty acres over to them so that they could put a manufactured home on their own property. After work, I'd just sink into the warmth of being with them, enjoying the sound of their laughter, and our quirky, insider family humor. One evening my mother, ninety years old by this point, came for a visit. She loved holding court, and especially having a captive audience to listen to her stories. But that evening, her sadness was palpable when she talked about being "the last one standing" in her generation. There was no one left to share her history, no one to remember what it was like seventy-five years earlier, when she had come of age. Her grief and sadness felt like a foreshadowing.

When the evening came to an end, I walked back to my studio and lingered on the deck. Looking out at the Milky Way glittering in a moonless sky, I waited for my Skype call with Tom. I felt sad at how quickly time devours decades of life. I was also poignantly aware of a gnawing feeling in my soul, hungry for life now, and hungry for life I had not yet lived.

WATCHING THE HOUSE TAKE SHAPE was like being part of an enormous, collaborative sculpture project. Every night when I got home from work, I'd change into jeans and a T-shirt and trot down to the job site. The crew would be gone, the sound of generator and power equipment silenced. With each week, my dream became more of a reality. Concrete piers were poured and spanned with four-by-fours. Beams, joists, and a plywood floor followed. Soon I could scramble up the ladder and walk the circumference.

By the time September rolled around, the workmen were building frames for the sliding glass doors. Our month of separation was coming to an end. The day before I left for Bolivia to join Tom, custom-built roof trusses were delivered on a big rig, with a crane on top of the cab. I watched it lower the main truss into place, spanning the forty-foot diameter of my house. Two men on ladders, one at each end, secured it to the weight-bearing posts. It was a miracle to behold.

The next morning, I woke at 6 a.m. and walked down the Bee Box Trail one last time. During the night, my "neighbors" had left clear messages in the soft dirt. The quail family had zigzagged everywhere, as if looking for direction. Tiny lizards made diminutive railroad tracks that crisscrossed the trail, and rabbit, squirrel, deer, and fox left their prints as well. The sun was just cresting the hills in the east as I came in sight of my glass house. What would it look like when I returned from Bolivia? All the sliding glass doors would be in place. The roof, sixteen triangular panels supported by a tall center post, would be covered in gleaming, silver metal. In my mind, it looked like a temple. Why not? Any dream that becomes a reality is sacred.

Chapter 26

I DROVE FROM CALAVERAS COUNTY to Berkeley on autopilot. The drive was so familiar. I pulled up in front of Tom's house the way I had seven months earlier, turned off the engine, and sat quietly, remembering that first morning. But the magnolia was no longer in bloom, no neighbor waved to me, wondering who I was, and Tom was not there. I was both leaning forward and pushing back, longing to be with my man and apprehensive at the same time. We'd been apart for four weeks, Skyping, emailing, and talking on the phone when we could, but it wasn't the same as being together. How would he feel when we met again? How would I feel? I planned to spend the night at Tom's and board my plane from San Francisco the next afternoon. With a two-hour layover in Dallas, I would arrive in La Paz the next morning.

I don't know how anyone sleeps on a red-eye curled up like a human pretzel. I squirmed through the night, wrestling with my tiny pillow and trying to cover up with a blanket the size of a beach towel, losing track of time in this economy-class purgatory. The flight attendant finally announced the arrival of morning by turning the cabin lights on. Warm washcloths were passed out, and something that barely passed as breakfast was served.

I felt exhausted and restless. I wanted to look beautiful for Tom. I wanted him to fall in love with me all over again. I grabbed a cosmetic bag out of my carry-on and lurched down the aisle toward the lavatory, hoping to do a makeover before we were to land in less than an hour. When the folding door closed behind me, I peered into the mirror. What I saw was not promising. My curly, silver-streaked brown hair looked like a fright wig. Wrinkles showed up where they hadn't been before, accentuated by dark circles under my eyes. My clothes looked as though I had slept in them, because I had. I brushed my teeth, washed my face, did the best I could to cover up the night's ravages, then returned to my seat as the captain announced, "Prepare for landing."

Tom was waiting for me at the curbside, standing beside a bright yellow taxi with the trunk open and the motor running. He said, "You arrived right on time," gave me a quick hug, and stowed my bag. I slid into the back seat and fastened my seat belt. I longed to hold him and cover his face with kisses, but I felt hesitant, not sure what to do next. In less than five minutes, we were driving through the outskirts of La Paz.

I turned to Tom and said "Hi," as if we hadn't been apart for a whole month. He put his arm around my shoulders and folded me into him. I could smell his clean, toasty scent and feel his warm breath in my hair. He whispered, "I love you so much. I missed you."

I said, "Me too," and knew that we were OK. It felt as if we were driving into the next phase of our life.

Our room was on the fourth floor of a modest stucco hotel just off Paseo El Prado. The color scheme was shades of red: burgundy brocade on the king-size bed, red velvet curtains, and hand-woven throw pillows in patterns of rust, magenta, and ochre. We turned down the bedspread and made sweet love, hungry for each other, then lay in each other's arms sharing the stories of our last forty-eight hours. Tom looked tired.

Living for a month at 12,000 feet while working nonstop, he'd been experiencing mild altitude sickness and had a bout of bronchitis. I held his head on my breast and stroked his hair, both of us at peace.

We walked into town for a light supper and returned to our room as night was falling. Tom was asleep before his head hit the pillow. I was overtired and lay awake, so I got up and pulled back the velvet curtains. The lights of La Paz were mirrored in the windows of a high-rise building directly across from us, glittering like a monolithic kaleidoscope. It was magic. I stood there for the longest time, feeling like all my molecules were finally coming together. I went back to bed and fell into a deep sleep.

During the night, a light rain washed the city clean. Sunday was a special holiday. Stores were closed and vehicles were banned from the streets. After breakfast at our hotel, we strolled down the Prado, a long avenue lined with tall buildings on either side. It had been transformed into a street fair, a mosaic of color, movement, music, and dancing. Vendors peddled sizzling, pungent sausages, popcorn, and snow cones in fluorescent colors of magenta, turquoise, lime green, and orange. Children were everywhere. In an improvised play space on the sidewalk, little ones stacked wooden blocks high until they crashed down to delighted squeals. Older kids played hopscotch, and teenagers skateboarded down steep streets empty of cars. Old men played chess on small metal tables set up in front of a café.

We heard a band playing raucous, happy music, surrounded by an audience of nearly one hundred people sitting in plastic chairs. People clapped in rhythm, but no one was dancing until a tiny, white-haired woman wearing a baseball cap and bright blue sweats turned to the woman next to her and invited her to dance. They clasped hands and tapped their feet, turning this way and that, in a folk dance they must have known all their lives. When the song ended, the audience burst into applause for the musicians and the two old women, who seemed utterly certain of their place in the dance and at home in their community. I clapped along with them and thought of my mother. These women were probably close to her age, in their nineties. And I thought about myself, wondering what it would be like to dance with abandon, at the center of a group of people who knew me so well.

When we returned to our hotel, Tom lay down for a nap. I needed quiet space and a shower. I could hear him snoring even before I got my clothes off. Standing naked under the hot water, I suddenly felt exhausted, completely drained, and fragmented, like a porcelain cup that had shattered on the tile floor. I started to shake, crying softly so I wouldn't wake Tom. *I'm in Bolivia for a month with the man I love. I'm seventy years old and I've found the love of my life. What the fuck is wrong with me?*

The answer came slowly. *I'm seventy years old. I want more time with Tom . . . more life.* When the crying stopped, I dried off and walked back into our bedroom. I climbed into bed next to Tom, curling my body into his. He mumbled something and put his arms around me.

I never told him about what happened as he lay sleeping that afternoon. At the time, I didn't understand. But in retrospect, I would see that it was about the two of us needing time to grow the relationship, and for me to learn to trust myself and Tom with these feelings. Even though we were not young, our love was. I kept my own counsel, not wanting to go more deeply into the shadows where my vulnerability hid. I thought, *Not now. Not on vacation.* But in truth, I knew I never wanted to go there.

TOM HAD SCHEDULED HIS TRIP to Charaña, a small town in the high desert, so I could go with him. I got to be the camera assistant, responsible for carrying the camera bag and tripod, handing him the right lens, making sure nothing was left behind, and staying out of the line of sight when he was filming. I felt inordinately proud of having this entry-level job, and I looked forward to seeing Tom at work.

We traveled eight hours by jeep to Charaña with a translator, our driver Daniel, and his girlfriend, in search of railroad tracks that, on Google Earth, were thin lines on the edge of a small village. Seventy-five years earlier, Tom's mother, Madeleine, took the train from Arica, Chile, to La Paz to join his father after he fled Europe. She had stopped at Charaña, the port of entry for all immigrants coming into Bolivia. We tracked her journey in reverse, pulling off the road whenever Tom wanted to film something his mother might have seen in this desolate country. I wondered what it was like for her, a woman traveling alone, to reunite with her beloved.

In loving her son, I felt a deep connection with her. I was experiencing Tom in a way I hadn't before, working at his craft, and wondered if she had known him as a filmmaker. It was a beautiful thing to see. When Tom was working, his focus was absolute, his relationship to the camera intimate. He moved with grace, panning a distant vista, holding his camera with a tenderness familiar to me when we made love. I began to see the world through his eyes, jagged mountain peaks etched in snow, silhouetted against billowing cumulus clouds, a river moving sinuously across the desert floor, a herd of vicuña, graceful as antelope and similar in color.

It was early evening when we saw Charaña in the distance, square adobe houses squatting in a grid on fine desert sand. The streets were empty. We followed what looked like a main street and discovered tracks on the edge of town, a railroad-crossing sign, and a boarded-up depot. Cinematically, we had hit pay dirt. Our companions went looking for some signs of life and a cold beer, while Tom and I shot footage for the next hour. When we met back at the jeep, our mates reported that a train ran once a week between Charaña and El Alto, a town just outside the La Paz city limits. We wanted to continue our exploration, but it was getting late. There was no food or lodging and the temperature at 14,000 feet was dropping fast.

A couple of miles out of town, Daniel turned onto a gravel road and stopped at a pile of boulders that hardly looked big enough to provide shelter, announcing that we would camp there. We unloaded the jeep and Tom and I set up our tent. Daniel collected sticks, started a small fire in a niche in the rocks, and began peeling onions, carrots, and potatoes for vegetable soup. A frigid wind was blowing so hard that our tent felt like the inside of a bellows. We put on every piece of clothing we had and stuffed ourselves into sleeping bags while waiting for supper. Finally, the hot soup was ready, and we gobbled it down with some crusty bread. After too many sleepless nights at high altitude, Tom took an Ambien and fell asleep. I tossed and turned, trying to get comfortable on the hard ground, hearing the wind raking every desiccated plant around us until I drifted off.

The wind died down in the night, and we woke up to morning stillness. Because we had a long drive back to La Paz, we packed up quickly while Daniel made us a breakfast of black tea and hot oat porridge. Two days later, we would be sleeping in a king-size bed in a five-star hotel in a historic colonial city.

After recovering from our overland journey to Charaña, we took an hour's flight over snowcapped Andean peaks to the dun-colored hills of Sucre. A taxi from the airport dropped us unceremoniously amid a throng of people. We were three long blocks from our hotel. Our driver's curt explanation: "Sorry, señor. The streets are closed. No cars, no taxis. It's the Virgin's festival." We were left standing next to our luggage and backpacks, wondering how we were going to get all this stuff to the hotel. Helpless in the moment to do anything, we looked at each other and laughed. I said, "It looks like we're in the middle of carnival. Might as well enjoy it."

A parade down the main boulevard pulsed with ecstatic energy. Groups of people wearing the traditional clothing of their villages performed regional dances. A troupe of young women, seductive in their ruby, emerald, and sapphire satin dresses, sparkling with sequins, strutted in front of a phalanx of miners, all wearing their headlamps, serious and proud. The miners slammed pickax handles on the ground to the rhythm of a band, self-consciously trying not to look at the girls.

We wove our way through the celebrants loaded down like pack animals, past Our Lady of Guadalupe Church, to our hotel, Parador Santa María La Real, a magnificent three-story former convent with a whitewashed facade that belied the opulence inside. We were welcomed by the doorman, who escorted us through an atrium with blue columns and yellow arches festooned with pink bougainvillea, to our room on the second floor. It was like walking through a time capsule into another world, serene and quiet, with curving wooden staircases, alcoves, and tiled balconies that opened to the city spread out below.

That afternoon, while Tom was on the phone making arrangements for a four-day trek into the mountains east of Sucre, I walked to the plaza across from the Virgin of Guadalupe church and sat on a bench next to two animated elderly ladies speaking Quechua. Although the plaza was filled with people, it was different from the festival the night before. Little kids rode tricycles on walkways that crisscrossed the plaza. Other kids kicked a soccer ball around the soft green grass. Teenagers made out surreptitiously on the outer perimeter of benches. Old women in worn-out bodies sold fresh-squeezed mandarin juice from wooden carts, and young girls screamed when boys tried to break in on their games. In two days, we would explore the countryside. I was ready for the kind of solitude trekking in nature brings, in a place I had never been before.

Chapter 27

THE NEXT MORNING, TOM WAS checking email and I was reading a book, just easing into the day. Our backpacks were by the door, ready for the trek that would begin in two days. We were in bed, propped up against pillows, when Tom said, "I just got an email from Richard in Berkeley. There's a fire in Calaveras County. They're calling it the Butte Fire."

I sat up, an alarm not yet sounding. "Butte is a town in Montana. Why would he send that to us?"

Tom's attention was focused on the screen. "I have no idea. Here, there's a link to a Cal Fire map."

I was looking over his shoulder when he pulled it up, zeroing in on my community of Mountain Ranch. Right in the center was a large area that looked like a bloodstain. In the center of the stain was my land, bounded by Michel Road, Old Gulch, and the town of Calaveritas. I could see the roads clearly and the BLM land that stretched for hundreds of acres beyond our southeast boundary.

Oh my God. Oh my God, oh my God. I couldn't think. My mind went into spasm. My heart began to pound. My throat clenched. I couldn't believe what I was seeing, right there, on Tom's laptop. Words wouldn't come. Tears wouldn't come. My mind was flooded with images—a forest on fire in blistering summer heat, flames licking up pine trees, dripping with sap from bark and cones, bone-dry manzanita and toyon bushes, ground cover so thick you couldn't walk through it. And what about my daughter, my son-in-law, his elderly father, and my grandson? Where were they? They had to be safe! I called Christa's cell phone, trying not to panic. No answer. It rang and rang and turned over to voicemail. *Lisa will know. Maybe they're safe with her in Sausalito.* Ring, ring, ring. *Lisa, answer the phone!*

"Hi, Mom. They're here. Everybody's here. Everybody's OK."

"They're safe? Oh my God, they're safe. Thanks, darling." Only then could I cry.

Christa came on the line. "Mom, don't cry. We're OK." She told me what happened. I listened without interrupting. "We had really hot weather after you left, in the high nineties, and wind. The fire started Wednesday afternoon. It spread fast from Moke Hill, not the town, but the land around it. On Thursday, we saw the smoke and smelled fire. Ash was falling everywhere. We had to evacuate immediately, and we threw everything we could into the car. We went to the Center in San Andreas, where we thought we would be safe. Grandma had to evacuate too, and she came to be with us. We all slept there overnight, but the fire kept spreading. Early in the morning, we could see flames on that ridge near the old cemetery, and were told again to evacuate, so we drove to Lisa's."

Christa was talking fast, trying to tell me what had happened and reassure me that they were safe, all at the same time. Her words seemed to smoosh together. It was hard to take it in. I had questions but couldn't formulate them. "What's important is that you guys are safe. I love you. Please tell everyone I love them. You're safe." And I began to cry again. Then I said, "I need to come home. . . . Should I come home?" I was hunched over a pillow, the phone glued to my ear, trying not to miss anything. I could feel Tom's hand in the center of my back, as if trying to hold me and steady me at the same time.

When Christa answered, her voice was flat, resolute. "There's nothing you can do. There's nothing anyone can do. Just think about it like you're evacuated to Bolivia. I'll text you as soon as we know something."

"Are our houses gone? Do you know?"

"It looks like they're all gone, but we won't know for sure until they get the fire under control and we can go home . . . if there is a home. I love you, Mom. Give Tom our love. Try to have your vacation."

Forest fires can burn fast and furious, covering miles a day. The Butte Fire was that kind of fire, a monster inferno on an unpredictable path, leaving total devastation in its wake. It struck our land and moved on. It would be a couple more days before we would know if anything had survived.

I woke up to sadness every morning after the fire, a great sadness, in Bolivia, in Sucre with my beloved. It was a time of sadness and joy. I slept a heavy sleep with dreams that weighed me down and no memory of them in the morning, coming into consciousness sometimes slowly, sometimes abruptly. When it was slow, I would roll into the warmth of my lover's body, my naked breasts against his naked back. Then the awakening was gentle and soft. When it was abrupt, words and images formed in my mind, incessant lists, inventories of things lost, and my small blue barn house, incongruously left standing in a dead world of ash and smoke.

I soon learned of the damage. Down our road, Christa and Bill's house survived, surrounded by acres and acres of death. It was unlivable. My studio was gone. The glass house, still under construction, was gone. My son's house was gone, a simple structure less than a quarter mile from us. It housed his and his wife's dreams for the future. Jim and Tanya had planned to retire there. It was now rubble. Unrecognizable shapes of things that once filled a family home were burnt and melted, fragments too broken to ever be put back together again. And what of dreams? Can dreams be put back together, or must they be dreamed anew?

We delayed our trek for a few days and walked the cobblestone streets of Sucre. I needed to grieve and to try to absorb what had happened thousands of miles and a world away. We sat in the plaza across from the church with the Virgin of Guadalupe watching over us. We talked, going more deeply into the mystery and magnificence, the darkness and the light, of each other's lives. We drank pisco sours and ate Bolivian food made indifferently for tourists in a dive bar late at night. We were learning to trust in ourselves, in the reality of our love for each other, and to seek peace at the center.

The days passed in a fog, and then it was time for our trek. Jaime, our guide, arrived at the Parador Santa María at 6 a.m. Packs and sticks were loaded into the back of an SUV, and Tom and I were whisked off to the trailhead, marked by a stone chapel dedicated to the Virgin. This early in the morning, no one was there but us. I was grateful that Jaime had left us alone in the chapel. It smelled of age and a few candles that had been left burning. Neither of us are Catholic, but the altar, a simple stone slab, beckoned. We lit two candles and placed them on the altar. I closed my eyes to pray—to whom? For what? Then a thought came: *You cannot replace a dead dream with an alive one.* My mind was strangely calm and attentive. *So now what? I'm a dreamer. How am I going to live?* I knew what dreams had died in the Butte Fire, but what dreams were still alive? There was no answer. Then I remembered Rilke's advice, to love the questions, and that sometimes we need to be willing to live into the answers. It felt like he was speaking directly to me.

It was getting warm, so we stuffed our fleece jackets into our packs, fitted the straps over our shoulders, fastened the hip belts, and followed Jaime. The earth was burnt sienna, yellow ochre, raw umber, and shades of white and gray. Ground cover, bushes, and scattered trees looked like relatives of the vegetation where I lived. The well-worn trail led down to a narrow gorge with a river running through it. Across the river, a sheer rock wall rose up, striped horizontally with sediment from life on Earth eons ago. We stopped there, hungry and lightheaded from the altitude. After lunch, Jaime asked Tom and me if we would like to try coca leaves, saying they would boost our energy. We answered yes, in unison. I told him that I was introduced to the sacred coca-leaf ritual on a trek in Peru. He smiled, nodded his head, and placed a large handful of leaves in each of our raised palms, along with a bit of the alkali chalk that acts as a catalyst. We chewed like contented cows, mesmerized by the patterns and colors of the cliff face, and then rose, shouldered our backpacks, and walked up the gorge. The afternoon passed in a meditative trance that the long trek (and the coca leaf) induced, and we arrived at dusk at our lodging, a small round earth house. After a dip in a nearby river and a simple supper, we fell sound asleep.

The next three days felt like time out of time. Perhaps the Virgin of Guadalupe was watching over us. We visited the studio of Adela, a Jalq'a weaver, and stayed with a friend of Jaime's, Doña Claudia, and her three children. Those two experiences would later stand out in my mind because they were distant from the hustle and commercialism of the cities. Both women opened their homes in ways that were healing to me.

On the afternoon of our second day, Adela's daughter welcomed us. She led us through their house, out the back door, and introduced her mother, a lean woman whose weathered face was focused on her loom. She sat on a pillow in the shade of courtyard walls, only interrupting her concentration to say hello and to invite us to join her. As her fingers flew across the loom, I knelt down to get a closer look at Adela's design, an underworld of darkness and chaos. Mythical creatures, known as *khurus*, were woven in red yarn, scattered randomly across a black background. The *khurus* resembled animals—horses, birds, snakes, and frogs—but they were disturbingly different, mutated. I saw no human figures.

Adela worked in silence for several minutes, then stopped to rest, saying that her eyes got easily tired. With Jaime translating, we learned that when Jalq'a women weave, images come to them in dreams, and their compositions emerge intuitively as they work. Adela was weaving a universal human story of the dark night of the soul, fear of the unknown, and the terrifying beings who inhabit the realm of nightmares. It was no wonder that I felt a strong connection to the images, and to the woman who wove them. Soon, I would be going home to a home that was no longer there. I was afraid to confront that reality. I had been compartmentalizing that realization so that I could be present with Tom in Bolivia, but the Butte Fire was a living nightmare. Christa texted pictures of the ruins of my studio and the glass house. Everything was burned beyond recognition. I knew that when I went home and actually saw the devastation, it would become my reality, and there would be nothing I could do to change it.

As we said goodbye to Adela, Tom asked about her eyes. Did she know why they were causing her pain? She looked up at all six feet six inches of him as if gauging why he would ask her such a question. Then she said matter-of-factly that her eyeglasses were broken. Tom thought for a moment and said, "I have an extra pair of readers. Do you want to try them?" She looked from Tom to Jaime as he translated and then back to Tom. She nodded, *Yes.* Tom took his reading glasses out of his shirt pocket and handed them to her. Adela perched them on her nose and stared at the weaving in front of her. For the first time since we arrived, a grin spread across her face. There was no need to translate.

EARLY IN THE EVENING ON THE last full day of our trek, we hiked down a dirt road to the home of Doña Claudia. Two young children burst through the front gate and came running to greet us. An older girl followed, trying to corral them as if they were frisky goats. The boy, Alejandro, was the youngest, maybe four years old, and in the lead. He leaped into Jaime's arms, talking excitedly in Quechua. Both girls hung back, looking shyly at us. Then Alejandro jumped down and raced across the yard, yelling for his mama in a flurry of dust, barking dogs, and squawking chickens. Doña Claudia came out of the house, wiping her hands on her apron, and greeted Jaime formally, shaking his hand and then ours. She gestured for us to lay our packs on a wooden picnic table under the covered patio. She told Jaime that the guesthouse was not ready. She would bring us some bottled water to drink. We should wait there.

It was good to rest. We watched the sun set below a distant mesa and listened to Doña Claudia and Jaime as they caught up with one another. Occasionally, Jaime would translate. Doña Claudia's husband was a laborer, working for a construction company in Sucre, and was gone for months at a time. It was the only way the family could survive financially. She had to manage their home and three children on her own. The oldest daughter was married, living in a neighboring village. Even though I did not understand Quechua, I could hear the defeat in her voice, and her fatigue. I thought about the young women we had seen in the parade, flaunting their beauty and their sexuality, eyes flashing, so sure of themselves. I wondered what had happened to Doña Claudia, living in rural Bolivia. I wondered what happened in her life, a woman barely forty, looking old enough to be her children's grandmother.

While Doña Claudia made dinner, Tom and I set to work, with Alejandro's help, sweeping the floor and dusting off the mattresses stacked against a far wall, so we would have a place to sleep. It looked as if the guesthouse hadn't been used in months. Just as we finished placing our mattresses together on the floor and laying our sleeping bags out, Doña Claudia called us for supper. The patio was illuminated by a single lightbulb. The table was set, and a simple meal of rice and boiled potatoes had been prepared, with a special green chili sauce made for the occasion of our visit. Jaime said that he also had something to share and brought out ripe, round oranges and a box of cookies left over from our lunch. While the kids peeled oranges and devoured the cookies, Tom placed his hands between the light and a whitewashed wall at the end of the table, making shapes with his fingers of a bird and a fox, complete with sound effects. When they came to life, the children squealed in delight. What magic! A story without words that was so simple and beautiful.

Our evening ended when the wind began to blow, bringing a light spattering of rain. Doña Claudia gathered up plates, silverware, empty serving dishes, and the children, bidding us *allin tuta*, good night in Quechua. We ran to the guesthouse for shelter and undressed modestly. Our bed was near the door. Jaime had discreetly placed his in the far corner. Soon both men were snoring, sounding like a Tom Waits duet. I was wide awake, listening to the rain drumming on the tin roof. Even the crash of thunder directly overhead and the flash of lightning just outside our window didn't wake them up.

A part of me wanted my evacuation in Bolivia to go on forever. The strangely out-of-body experience of both knowing and not knowing what I would be going home to was a kind of respite. Once you know something, you can't unknow it.

Chapter 28

WE RETURNED TO SUCRE FOR a few days, then back to La Paz long enough to collect Tom's camera equipment. We flew home to Berkeley, Tom's home, on a Friday. But where was my home? We gave ourselves the weekend to wind down, all the while knowing that on Monday, we would drive to Calaveras County, to what was left after the Butte Fire.

The drive up Mountain Ranch Road was so familiar. Although we were inexorably moving toward something that had already happened, I knew that seeing it would make it real. I closed my eyes and began to imagine the hospital on my right, the turn toward Calaveritas, the vineyard, Rocky Road bridge, and Mark Maithre's place.

You have to see what's there. You're not a child. Closing your eyes won't make it go away. Fuck. I willed my eyes to open. We had only driven a quarter of a mile.

Tom said, "You OK?"

"No." My voice was so quiet, it was hard to hear myself.

"I'm here," he reassured me.

"Yeah, I know. Thank you. I love you."

"I love you too."

Then I saw the green. My eyes drank it in. Trees, lots of green trees, and black oaks starting to turn gold, a few houses, an old barn, somebody's tractor parked next to a carport. My heart was beating hard, my breath audible. I knew there was a place on this drive up the mountain where my world would be gone. I just didn't know where exactly. I willed my eyes to stay open. Then it was there, and then it filled my eyes with tears, and then I couldn't see for a while.

How can you still feel while going numb? My eyes were open the whole time, but I wouldn't remember the drive. We parked near the house. Everything was burned up, as far as I could see, everywhere ash-like gray powder and the blackened bones of trees. My truck was a rusted hulk, windows blown out, kneeling on rims in a hardened pool of melted rubber. Fallen power lines dangled from burnt poles. Nothing was left of the old power shed but cinderblock walls. Even the water tank had melted. My little barn house had survived. Painted a beautiful teal blue, it looked absurd, like a colorful toy left in a junkyard. And Christa and Bill's place just down the road? How could it still be there? I imagined the fire spinning around it in a dervish dance, driven by the unrelenting force of the wind.

We walked holding hands to my studio. My studio. I was looking at the remains of a cremation. Have you ever held the ashes of someone you loved in your hands? I held my dad's when I scattered them just a few yards from where I was standing. I was surprised that they were like chalk, like coarse beach sand with small fragments of bone.

At first, all that seemed to be left of my studio was the twisted metal roof and wood-burning stove, lying where they had collapsed. I picked through the debris. I didn't know what I was looking for, but I squatted on the ground, searching. Then I saw something I couldn't believe. Where my bookshelf had been, a book was lying open, the pages bound, as if I had been reading it before I left for Bolivia. But all the words were gone, burned away by the fire. Each page looked intact but was reduced to ash. Each perfect page fell apart at my touch. I stood up and hugged myself, sobbing. *There were no words. No words . . .*

Chapter 29

WE'D BEEN HOME FOR A COUPLE of weeks, resuming our bifurcated life, sharing Tom's home Friday through Monday. On Tuesday mornings, I drove to my office in Calaveras County, worked through Thursday, then drove back to Berkeley. I stayed in the barn house on Tuesday and Wednesday nights. On those nights, my only companion was Smokey, my feral cat, who had miraculously survived the fire. In no way was Smokey a house cat, but we were attached. She would come out of nowhere to greet me when she heard my car drive up the dirt road at night, and in the early morning, when I'd take my cup of tea outside to watch the sunrise, she would try to leap into my lap before I could sit down.

I had no water and no electricity. After the fire, the county building department had refused to allow power to be restored to homes like mine that were livable but had been built before the fire without permits. I had a wood-burning stove for heat, propane for the range and refrigerator, and bottled water. I felt defiant about living there, rationalizing that I could live rough because I could backpack in the wilderness for days at a time.

Friends and family had offered for me to stay with them, but I felt like I had to do this on my own. This was my home. It had survived. It looked so forlorn on the burned-up land that I couldn't abandon it. I couldn't shake off this sense of loyalty to my small house and my responsibility to care for it. It felt as if we were all survivors, Smokey, my house, and me.

The house had started as a simple barn with a gable roof, one window, and a barn door. It was adequate as a rustic weekend live-work studio. Remodeling an outbuilding to make it livable was not uncommon in Calaveras County on property tucked away in the hills. It's called "guerrilla building" if you do it without permits. After my divorce, it was the only way I could afford to have a home again. Family, friends, and neighbors helped with the construction. Some got paid and some worked for love. Four generations of my family did the framing. My mother was part of the crew, and my grandkids pounded nails at whatever height they could reach. It felt as if the bones of my house were ancestral. The barn was completed according to code, inspected, and signed off. I didn't consult with the building department when, over time, amenities were added—French doors and windows, wood paneling, and indoor plumbing. The hayloft became a bedroom with a spiral staircase. I planned to live out my life on that land in that small house. I didn't plan on the Butte Fire.

One Sunday morning in Berkeley, I woke up before Tom, feeling calmer. I could feel my heart beating quietly in my chest. The thought *Choose life* was as clear as if I had spoken it out loud. Padding out to the kitchen in bare feet, I brewed a cup of Russian Caravan tea. It smelled like burning wood and tobacco. I drank it down.

Choose life.

With an image of the blank pages of my art books filling the screen in my mind, all the words burned away, I wandered into my makeshift studio, a converted bedroom in Tom's house.

There was a desk and a big worktable, a huge office chair that was Tom-size, a metal wastebasket, and an empty bookshelf. I was grateful for the studio, but there was nothing on the walls, no art of mine. *You cannot rebuild the life you had from charred fragments of memory. You have to build something new.* Then I heard Tom's voice in my mind, singing a song he loves by Pat Humphries.

> *We are living 'neath the great Big Dipper*
> *We are washed by the very same rain*
> *We are swimming in this stream together*
> *Some in power and some in pain*
> *We can worship this ground we walk on*
> *Cherishing the beings we live beside*
> *Loving spirits will live forever*
> *We're all swimming to the other side.*

I realized that since the fire, I'd been swimming in loss with no sense of direction. That morning I woke up on the other side. *I choose life.*

I'D BEEN LIVING ON THE BURNED LAND for three weeks. It was mid-October and getting dark when I got home. I had to find my way around with a flashlight. Cooking dinner by the light from candles and a battery-operated lantern was challenging. On the last night before returning to Berkeley, I felt especially fragile in the enveloping blackness just outside the four walls of my house. Dinner was simple, a burrito with everything for a balanced meal wrapped into a flour tortilla. I'd diced tomatoes, black olives, and an avocado on the kitchen table. Turning back to my piles after checking to see if the black beans in a pot on the stove were hot enough, I smelled something burning. My hair. *Fuck! My hair is on fire!*

I grabbed a towel from the counter and frantically slapped it against my forehead. It only took a couple of seconds to smother the fire, but I was shaking and sobbing, trying to find my way to the bathroom with a flashlight to assess the damage. Even though it wasn't so bad, just singed hair framing my stricken face, I felt sad and scared and ashamed all at the same time. A familiar voice in my mind said, *This is on you. You broke the rules when you built this house. It's your responsibility, so live with it.*

After a solemn dinner, I called Tom to tell him what had happened. He was upset. "You can't live there. We'll figure out what to do next, but right now I'm going to call the Eagles and ask if you can stay at their place." Tom phoned our friends who lived farther up the mountain. They said yes without hesitation, so the next week, I began spending Tuesday and Wednesday nights with them.

Chapter 30

THREE MONTHS LATER, WE STILL didn't have a long-range plan. Commuting from Berkeley every week, living with friends when I was in Calaveras County, there was no space or time. It was overwhelming to work with clients traumatized by the fire, many of whom had lost everything, as well as dealing with the insurance company, county building department, FEMA, the Small Business Administration, and lawyers. At other stuck times in my life, I learned that when you don't know what to do, do nothing. Just wait. So we waited.

December 10, 2015, would become a kind of anniversary. It was the day that Tom figured out what to do next. He was driving from Berkeley to spend a long weekend with me. We planned to meet at my office, then drive together some twenty miles to the home of a second couple I was staying with. I had finished my last session and was gathering up my stuff when I heard Tom coming up the stairs. I was so excited to see him that I flung the door open and hugged him before he could cross the threshold into my office.

"Let's talk." His tone was serious. "There's something I want to discuss with you."

My stomach lurched. I thought, *Oh shit! Something really is wrong.* We sat on the couch, and he told me about the epiphany he had had while driving across the delta.

"I was thinking about our situation and had an idea. I could sell my house in Berkeley. The equity would be enough to buy a house here, and I would be mortgage-free. Then we could live together, not this bifurcated thing." He was looking at me earnestly, his sentences short and to the point. "Your work is here, but my home base can be anywhere. It sounded so crazy, even to me, that I called Dick and told him what I just told you. I said, 'This is nuts, right?' He's my closest friend, and he said, 'You and Sharon love each other. It's a no-brainer. I think it's a good idea.'"

Then Tom looked into my eyes and asked, "What do you think?"

What do I think? It was hard to catch my breath, to take in the full meaning of what he was saying. It was an incredibly wonderful, crazy, beautiful idea. I held Tom's face gently, tears streaming down my face. *We could have a life together. Here. This man loves me.* I had the sensation in that moment that the love I felt for Tom was spilling out between my fingers. I said, "Yes, my darling, yes. You would do this for us? I love you so much . . ." and then we held each other, laughing and crying. Together, we could choose what came next.

MY FRIENDS, JAN AND JOHANNA, were waiting for us when we arrived at their house. They had a fire going in their woodstove and wine and cheese on the coffee table in front of an overstuffed couch. Their two enormous shaggy white dogs came bounding out to greet us as we got out of the car, barking a warning and wagging their tails at the same time. They knew me, but not the tall guy walking up to the gate with me. Tom was introduced all around. We went into the warmth of the house and sat around the table. Tom's first visit was toasted with wine. After the toast, Jan turned to Tom and asked in her no-nonsense way, "So, what's this I hear about your bifurcated life? How's it goin'?"

Tom, also direct, answered, "Well, it's not working very well for either of us . . . I have this plan," and he proceeded to tell her what he'd shared with me.

Before he could finish, Jan leaned in with a smug look of satisfaction on her face and announced that she had the perfect house for us. "Some friends of mine in Angels Camp built a straw-bale house maybe twenty years ago. It's up for sale. I'll call them and see if it's still on the market."

She was out of her chair and heading for the phone hanging on the wall before Tom and I gave each other an affirmative look and he said, "Yeah. Let's see if it's available." Jan was like that. All it took was one call.

She came back, sat down, and said, "We're good to go. Tomorrow morning at ten."

WE PULLED UP IN FRONT OF A single-story bungalow that looked like a French country house, with yellow ochre walls the texture of adobe and French windows with shutters and trim in a deep cerulean blue. It was on twenty acres of rolling hills dotted with oaks and gray pine. Jan knocked soundly on the heavy oak front door and introduced us to a couple in their eighties. The husband invited us to make ourselves at home and feel free to look around. No realtors were there. No sales pitch.

I stood still and absorbed the energy. A straw-bale house is like no other kind of structure. Although the ceilings were ten feet high and the rooms spacious, the house had an organic, womblike feel, as if it had been grown and not built. No corners were squared off, and no walls perfectly straight. I felt held in the space. I looked over at Tom, standing a few feet away. His attention seemed as rapt as mine. Windows and doors with glass panes were on the south and east side, to let the warmth of the sun in during the fall and winter months. With curtains and drapes gone, it would be like a glass house. I counted ten doors as Tom and I walked through the house. Whoever had heard of ten outside doors in one house? I loved it. No matter what room you were in, you could step outside.

We talked about what it would be like to live there. We envisioned Tom's office and mine, a guest room, and where the art would hang. There was even an enclosed breezeway that would be a perfect, spacious art studio. By the time we made our way out to the brick patio with its breathtaking view of hills and farmland, we knew this would be our home. Three days later, our offer was accepted, and we were in escrow. We moved in less than a month later on January 7. A new year, a new beginning.

Chapter 31

MOVING IN TOGETHER FELT LIKE two kids playing house, only we were grown-ups with a house of our own. Choosing furniture was easy. Mine had burned up. Both of us liked Tom's eight-foot sofa; roomy side chairs; the ash dining room table he had built decades before; an art deco chair we found discarded on a Berkeley sidewalk, reupholstered in red leather; and our king-size bed. Having decided not to hang art we didn't absolutely love, we discovered that our combined, eclectic collection of paintings, photographs, and art masks lived well together. It seemed like another good omen, but there was a shadow over our connubial bliss.

I had lived in Calaveras County for fifteen years. When I moved from Berkeley in 2000, George W. Bush and Al Gore were running for president. Bush signs were posted everywhere on fence posts and in people's front yards, alongside small American flags. I flaunted a "Get Out the Bushes" bumper sticker like a political chip on my shoulder, and I seriously wondered if I could live in this conservative Republican community. But over time, I found my own tribe of liberal folks, most of them expats from the Bay Area, and came to appreciate a diversity that was very different from what I experienced in Berkeley.

Now Tom was having his own process of acculturation. He kept busy doing projects, converting the front bedroom into his office and building storage space for professional equipment and his archive of documentary films while learning how to maintain our well, septic, and supplementary solar system.

I'd overhear him talking with city friends about living in "the boonies," entertaining them with his stories of country life, until I told him that characterization hurt my feelings. "This isn't the boonies. We live here, and it takes time to get to know people. Just give it a chance before you decide." What I really meant was "give us a chance." I was taking it personally, even though I understood how hard it was for Tom to feel so isolated. He was used to walking five minutes to his favorite café and spending the afternoon on his laptop, surrounded by the sounds of others working or talking quietly. You couldn't even see the nearest neighbors from our property, and the only Starbucks was twenty minutes away by car. I didn't tell him that sometimes I felt responsible when he was unhappy, afraid he would regret the move—and me. I didn't even want to acknowledge it to myself.

A month later, when I was at work, Tom was moving an eight-foot-high storage unit he had just finished building when he lost his balance and tweaked his back. When I got home, he was sitting in his recliner in the dark. I flipped on the light and asked, "What's wrong, darling? Are you OK?"

Tom looked sideways at me with real pain in his eyes. "I've hurt my back."

"Oh no, how bad is it?"

"I'm icing it and I took five ibuprofen, but it's barely touching the pain."

I pulled a chair close to him and asked, "What can I do to help?"

"There's a leftover prescription of hydrocodone in the medicine cabinet.

Can you bring me one with a glass of water?"

That was the beginning of a full year of back pain: urgent care visit the following morning, X-rays, MD consult, physical therapy, and assorted trials of pain medicine. Surgery was contraindicated, so we tried three different chiropractors until we found one who treated the whole body and its relationship to the injured area. After months of treatment, Tom's back began to get better, but pain was still an issue.

We made new friends. Old friends came for weekends. We loved taking walks with them on the land, making meals together, and drinking mulled wine in the hot tub in the last chill days of winter. We decided to have an open house in May with all of our friends and family, to celebrate our love with the people we loved. We drew up a list of forty guests and imagined them sitting with us in a circle beneath the gnarled oak tree that greeted everyone who came to our home. After a ceremony we couldn't yet envision, we'd share a sumptuous meal.

This wasn't going to be a potluck and we didn't want to cook, so we scheduled a meeting with the chef of a local restaurant known for its unique menu and catering. When we arrived and looked around the empty dining room with wooden tables and benches for seating, we wondered if we'd come to the wrong place. A burly bearded man in scruffy jeans and a flannel shirt came out from the kitchen and said gruffly, "Hi. I'm Craig. What can I do for you?" as if we'd interrupted him.

Tom struggled to describe our event. "Well, it's a celebration. Uh, we've been together for a year and a half, and we want to honor our relationship . . . with our friends—"

Craig interrupted, "Sounds like you're getting married."

His observation hung in the air. Tom looked at me and slowly smiled as if in recognition of something that was obvious. "Yeah, I guess we are." Then he paused, searching for the right words, and said, "It's a marriage ritual." He took my hand under the table, and for the rest of the meeting held onto it.

I felt the way Tom did about the word *marriage*. We had each married and divorced three times. It came with too much baggage, too much heartache, and a sense of failure. I wondered if I was more cynical than he was. For years, the Tina Turner song "What's Love Got to Do with It?" played in my mind like a mantra. I knew from experience that a real marriage had to be created every day by both people. One person couldn't do it alone, and it wasn't about a piece of paper. I'd learned the hard way that a marriage license was most relevant during the divorce. Tom and I had already executed the other legal documents that people our age in committed relationships needed. We didn't want a contract. The word we chose was *covenant*, and we wrote our vows in the spirit of love, not obligation.

ON MAY 14, 2016, OUR COMMUNITY gathered around. We shared our vows under the old oak tree.

Tom began, "Sharon, my love, this love between us is not like any I have experienced before. It is not a contract, an assignment of roles, or an affirmation that everything will 'turn out right in the end.' It is not safe. It is not 'preordained' or 'meant to be.' It is both light and dark . . . a yearning, a thirsting of the soul that is slaked each day in unexpected ways. It is the active work of trial and error, of learning and practicing a way of fitting together, joyfully. Love requires courage."

He included a quote from Annie Dillard about how it was so easy to "simply step aside from the gaps where the creeks and the winds pour down," saying, "I never merited this grace . . . the world is wilder than that in all directions, more dangerous and bitter, more extravagant and bright." He concluded with, "I love you, Sharon. I want to be your husband. I want to love you as my wife. Let us go into the gaps together with our friends' blessing."

I responded, "Tom, my heart is full of love for you, and gratitude for the grace that has brought us together. You are the love of my life. Today, I choose you as my husband, and I choose to be your wife, as if for the first time. It is not an act of possessiveness, but a gift freely given, with a depth of understanding of what that means. I have no need to promise to love you in some future moment. Would I promise to give you the gift of my breath or the beating of my heart? You are so close to me that our life has its own pulse. It is always there. Who am I now, this woman who loves you, and who are you, my beloved? Let's continue to find out together in the shelter of our love, in the nakedness of our love, in the darkness and the light."

Then we invited our friends to tell their stories of love in our circle. We toasted and shared a simple, elegant meal. After saying good night to our guests, Tom and I sat together in the quiet of our living room, blissfully exhausted. We felt held in the circle of love that was our marriage celebration. We had vowed to love each other in darkness and in light, to go into the gaps together. It was a treasured moment. There was no way we could have known that only one week later, our vows would be tested beyond what either of us could imagine.

Chapter 32

THE DAY AFTER OUR CELEBRATION, Tom collapsed into a dark, frightening depression. He had kept the back pain at bay with meds, the balm of our close community, and sheer will, but at 3 a.m., he was in despair. I turned toward him in bed and asked, "Are you OK?" He told me that pain had kept him awake most of the night. He was afraid there would be no end to it. What awaited him when he got out of bed felt like an impenetrable wall.

Tom had begun his book, *The Restless Hungarian*, two years before we met. Around the time we moved to Angels Camp, the focus of his work became deeply personal. He was writing about growing up with his schizophrenic mother after his parents' divorce and his sister's suicide when he was a teenager. He knew that he could not bring their stories to life from the objective point of view of a journalist. He had to relive what it was like for them, and for him as a child. I remembered his father's drawings, particularly the portraits of his mother in a kind of time-lapse sequence, showing her descent into madness. I rolled onto my side and said, "Please talk to me."

He lay motionless on the bed, staring up at the ceiling. His voice was flat, the words parsed out with no emotion. The story was familiar. Tom had shared it with me early in our relationship, but I could hear a tone of hopelessness that hadn't been there before. I felt apprehensive and drew my knees up to my chest self-protectively. "The way I survived my mother's insanity was to hate her, to completely separate myself from her, but in the past months, I've come to see her in a different light. Before I was born, my mother wrote love letters to my father. When I read them, I saw this whole other person before her sickness. I felt compassion for her. I felt love for my mother. Then I had to write about what it was like to be a really scared boy, alone with her, while she was going crazy. To hold these two things, the love and the hate, and not run screaming from my desk, was really hard. As a child, I learned that to be loved by my mother, I had to accept her fearful perception of a hostile world. But I knew that if I did that, I would go crazy too."

I stroked his hair, murmuring "Shhhh, shhh. I'm here. You're going to be OK," but a sense of apprehension settled in my gut. Tom had reached an emotional and physical saturation point. Reexperiencing his family tragedy, while still in pain from the back injury, was overwhelming his capacity to cope. Now he was afraid he would succumb to schizophrenia, like his mother. I leaned over to hold him. His body relaxed into mine. Both of us were crying. After a while, I fixed breakfast. It was a workday for me, but I rescheduled my clients. We worked on our own projects, stopping at midday to take a coffee break together and a walk. This felt strangely normal and momentous at the same time.

Tom seemed more stable for the next couple of days, staying immobile as much as he could to manage the physical pain while continuing to write. He reconnected with his psychologist of many years in Berkeley, agreeing to weekly phone sessions. I returned to my office, grateful for my time with clients and being able to focus on their lives instead of my own.

During those first days in crisis with Tom, there was no space for what was building up in me, but I could feel the pressure. The only time I had alone was on my commute, so I tried counseling myself on the way to work, discussing my issues dispassionately, as if I was conducting my own case conference. I started by naming the fear that seemed to be encroaching on my own sanity. Abandonment. I wanted to demolish the fear and the shame that went with it. Next was a discussion of my family of origin. I reported the facts as if they belonged to someone else: *Growing up, I felt unlovable. I had two narcissistic parents who were emotionally and physically absent. Assorted aunts and uncles, other kids' moms, and babysitters cared for my brother and me. We felt we didn't belong anywhere. I learned not to have any needs my parents couldn't meet, never to ask for help, and to perform well at school to get attention. As an adult, fear of being abandoned got entangled with "love." Having expectations was unthinkable, because having them fulfilled was unimaginable. I chose narcissistic men, trying to get love they were incapable of giving, and then abandoning them before they could abandon me.*

As I drove into the parking lot, I realized that my session with myself hadn't worked. I could not be my own therapist. I felt scared both for Tom and for me. I didn't know what to do with my fear and growing sense of hopelessness. I couldn't discuss it with Tom. He was too fragile. I didn't know how to help myself and didn't feel comfortable talking to friends. How could I share what was going on with me without talking about what was happening with Tom? That was his story to tell. Confidentiality is a big deal to me. It is crucial in any therapeutic relationship and equally so with family and in friendships. What we were going through felt too intimate, and too private, to discuss outside our relationship. So I held it together for two days. Then I cracked.

It was Friday. Tom sat at the breakfast counter watching me fix lunch. We were making small talk, easing into our long weekend, when the tortilla chips I was toasting under the broiler burst into flames. I opened the door, calmly extinguished the fire with a lid, and put the smoking mess outside on the patio. When I came back inside, continuing our conversation, Tom pointed at the stove and said with an edge in his voice, "The soup is boiling over!"

What I heard was, *Can't you do anything right?* He just sat there doing nothing. I turned the heat off in time, but something snapped in my mind. It went blank. It was as if I was fourteen years old, alone in my bedroom. I felt trapped and desperate to find something to break, to throw against the wall, to shatter something of mine. I needed to break free of me. Then I became aware of Tom looking at me, quiet and watchful. I told him that when I was a kid, if I was scared and didn't know how to comfort myself, I broke things. The wall in my bedroom looked as if it had been hit by blasts from a shotgun. It was there in plain sight, but no one ever asked what was wrong. As an adult I understood that it was a cry for help, to be seen, to be heard, but in my family, there was no seeing, no hearing, no comfort. I had learned to transmute fear into anger. It felt more powerful, and I acted it out in a way that hurt no one but me.

Tom asked gently, "Do you need to do this now, to break something?" I felt suspended in time, dangling at the end of his question.

I said, "Yes," and then I reenacted my private ritual with Tom as my witness. Prowling around the living room, I searched for an object to break, something I loved. I found an exquisite blown-glass sculpture that looked like a sea anemone before it opens and bolted out of the house with it. Tom followed. I stopped for a moment, feeling tears stuck in my throat. Then I smashed it on the front-entry bricks. My mind immediately condemned me. *You did this. You did this shameful, private thing. You did this in front of Tom.* I ran through the house to our bedroom. Our bed was safe. I curled into a ball around the shame in my belly, sobbing in anguish and humiliation.

Tom came to me. "I love you. I'm here for you."

I wanted him to hold me, but a scared child inside said no. The angry teenager, her eyes blazing, shouted, "*There is no safe place!*" and then a very young voice whispered, "I'm afraid. I don't want to be alone anymore."

TWO DAYS LATER, ONLY ONE WEEK after our marriage ritual, I woke up with a heavy weight upon my shoulders, condensed into two tight knots at the base of my neck. Tom's side of our bed was empty. I got up, still half asleep, and wandered through the house looking for him. There was a short note on the dining room table, hastily written in Tom's familiar scrawl: "Woke up at 6:30. Couldn't go back to sleep. Went for a walk. Love you."

I felt a little uneasy, unable to alleviate my fear. I brewed a pot of coffee, sat at the dining room table trying to read the latest *New Yorker*, and waited. When Tom walked in, I got up to give him a kiss, but I stopped when I saw his face. It looked collapsed. He said yes to a cup of coffee and sat down heavily in his recliner. When I joined him, his words were barely audible. "I need to tell you something," he said.

I felt the fear lodged in my gut spike. "OK, sweetheart."

The look in his eyes was frightening. "I've been thinking about killing myself. It terrifies me. Usually going for a walk helps, but not this morning. I didn't want to tell you, because I didn't want to scare you. The last few days I can't seem to get the thought out of my head."

I knew that Tom had experienced bouts of depression since childhood, and that he was struggling now, but he had never before talked about suicide. I wanted to put my hands over my ears and scream, *No! No, no, no! This is too much!* but I knew I couldn't do that. Suddenly the psychologist in me went on high alert.

I said, "My darling, you needed to tell me. I'm here. You're safe." I had to set the frightened wife aside to do a risk assessment of my husband. Everything slowed down. I felt a rhythm inside of me, breathing in and breathing out, holding attention in a focused but soft way. I listened for direction. It was familiar to me, this interior experience. I trusted it. In the gentlest way, I asked, "Can you tell me if you've had thoughts about how you might do this?"

"Yes, driving my car fast into a big tree . . . taking all my medications . . . buying a gun." He was trembling. "I feel so ashamed."

I touched his hand and said quietly, "You need to tell me all of this. You're doing so good."

I could feel a lump in my throat, tears I could not shed, and a roiling in my stomach that came in waves. "I need to ask a couple more questions to be sure you're safe." He nodded. "Do you have any intention of hurting yourself?"

"No. I want to live. I just don't know how anymore."

"That's good, darling. It's important to know that. It's also important for us to have a 'No Harm' contract. You and me. Do you know what that is?" He shook his head no, looking in my eyes searchingly. "It means you agree to tell me if you have any serious thoughts about harming yourself, to talk to me, before acting on any of those thoughts. Do you agree?"

"Yes. Do you think I need to be hospitalized?"

This question had been in my mind from the moment Tom had said, "I've been thinking about killing myself." Tom had asked for help and was open to receiving it. I could feel his body relax as we talked. His voice had become softer; his words flowed more easily. He made eye contact with me, and I could see color returning to his face as we talked. When he said he had no intent, that he wanted to live, and agreed without hesitation to a "No Harm" contract, I knew that his healing had already begun. He had support from me, a strong therapeutic relationship with his psychologist, and work that he believed in. My answer was, "I don't think so, but we need to call your therapist."

Tom's psychologist also agreed that hospitalization wasn't necessary. He said he could work with us as a couple, and with Tom in individual sessions, if that would be supportive. I think we said yes in unison. I was becoming exhausted trying to hold Tom's grief and fear and my own. We both felt incredibly grateful for this offer of help.

After we hung up, I started to cry. The therapist in me had done her job. Now I needed Tom to hold me, his wife, lover, and friend, and so did a small child inside of me. She had come back from a very dark place where nothing existed but emptiness and terror, sobbing, "Don't go away. Please don't leave me." Tom rocked me back and forth in his recliner, saying, "I'm not going to leave. I'm here. I won't abandon you." I sucked his words in like oxygen. For the moment, I could breathe. But frightening questions that I had no answers for spun in my mind.

Tom was suicidal. He told me the terrifying thoughts about ending his life, but over and over, I asked myself, *How could this be?* We had been deeply in love for a year and a half. We had supported each other through the devastation of the Butte Fire and started over again in Angels Camp. Only seven days earlier, we celebrated our love in a marriage ritual. It seemed that somehow, in the enveloping safety of our love, the wild beasts of childhood had been unleashed and now roamed the land of our psyches. Each of us had spent an adult lifetime securing the locks on their cages, examining them in therapy from a relatively safe distance. Now there was no safety, and the beasts were small, terrified captives, our inner children. We were trying to hold and soothe them. They were trying to be comforted. We were exhausted. It felt as though each of us had hit an emotional, psychological, and spiritual bottom.

The next four months, Tom and I lived on two levels of consciousness, our professional lives in the outer world and our inner world healing from childhood trauma. We came to better understand this love that was both sensitive and ruthless, tender and violent, a love that shredded the survival strategies we had learned as kids. It left us feeling naked, vulnerable, and at times weak with fear. The very nature of our love, the safety we felt being together, had allowed this to come forward. We called it our dark night of the soul, continuing to question what it demanded of us. Faith? Faith in what? God? My word for God was *Life*, the cycle of life that embraces everything, so I started there. Trusting life. Trusting Tom. Trusting myself. It had to be enough.

We made plans for the end of summer, a flight to Boston on September 9, 2016, one year after the Butte Fire, and then one glorious month to live, work, and play in the house designed and built by Tom's father on Cape Cod where he'd spent every summer of his boyhood. We couldn't wait.

Chapter 33

THE NIGHT BEFORE FLYING TO CAPE COD, I dreamed I was swimming in a river with a community of people. Tall stone structures with stained-glass windows and winding staircases stood like sacred formations in the river. The fast-moving water flowed effortlessly around them, as did we. I told my companions, "You know, you can fly," and I soared up out of the water, my arms swimming through the air. I felt free.

Boarding the plane the next day, I felt anything but free. A month in Cape Cod with no responsibilities was an unopened gift. I couldn't imagine what might be inside. Tom and I seemed like survivors being given a place of comfort and time to heal. It was freedom, but I didn't know what to do with it. We had gone through too many crises in too short a time with not enough space to grieve. I clung to the blessings we experienced along the way like a life raft, but I was also afraid of losing them. And I was acutely aware of the absence of my muse, a constant companion since childhood. She had always been there, this intimate part of myself, giving expression to what I saw and felt but couldn't articulate. Through painting, drawing, and sculpting, we made art out of whatever was available.

As I got older and more fluent with words, writing became an additional voice. Into this hollow space, I silently cried out, *Who can I trust now?* The response came back like an echo: *Trust yourself. Trust Tom. Trust life.*

I decided to go to Cape Cod packing nothing but my clothes. No art materials. No books. No expectations. I wanted a new beginning. I told Tom on the way to the airport that if I could go naked, I would.

The two-hour drive from Boston to Wellfleet, to Tom's childhood summer home, was magical. I had never before been to New England. Lush green foliage contrasted with the dun-colored hills, parched manzanita, and sunburned oaks we had left behind. It was like taking a cold drink with my eyes. We were driving on the Pilgrims Highway. The name fit perfectly. I began to feel that first stirring of adrenaline, so familiar to me at other times on other journeys. It always started at the trailhead, leaving behind what was familiar for untrodden territory.

Turning off the highway, we followed a winding road, past weathered Cape Cod–style houses. Each one had a gabled roof, shuttered windows on either side of a door placed front and center, and a chimney on top. They looked like charming children's drawings. Tom got quiet when we turned off Pilgrims Highway onto a country road that branched off like the limbs of a tree. At each juncture, hand-lettered signs with family names were posted. Tom said, "Ours disappeared a long time ago. I've got to pay attention, so I don't miss the turn." I sensed his anxiety as well as my own. It felt a little bit like anticipating Christmas morning, wondering what presents would be mine, afraid of being disappointed.

And suddenly it was there, the house Tom's father had built, suspended in space between earth and sky, balancing on slender stilts. The single-story design was elegant in its simplicity. There were no stairs leading up to the front door. Instead, a delicate ramp beckoned us into the house as if it were a continuation of the road. Tom had talked to me months before about his father's passion for "the joy of space," but I hadn't fully understood it until now. When we unlocked the door and stepped inside, floor-to-ceiling windows on the north and east walls banished any sense of separation from the surrounding forest and the pond just a few yards away. The interior space was open. The living room flowed into a dining area, separated from the kitchen by a low counter with a swinging door. A few pieces of modernist furniture—couch, coffee table, and an assortment of chairs—cast shadows on the hardwood floor. Bookshelves lined one wall next to a fireplace already laid with logs. We were home.

Chapter 34

WHEN I SAW HIGGINS POND FOR the first time, I fantasized about rolling out of bed before breakfast and skinny-dipping. The next morning, as sunlight evaporated the mist rising from the pond, I whispered in Tom's ear, "Hey. Let's go for a swim. Come on, the day's too beautiful to stay in bed." He mumbled something incoherent and rolled over, so I shook him gently. "You'll be very sad if you don't go."

He sat up, rubbing sleep out of his eyes, and said, "OK. You win. Let's do it."

We walked barefoot to the beach on a carpet of dry pine needles, through the narrow opening in a hedge that circled the pond like a scraggly mustache. Tom strode into the water and dove in, but I wanted to savor this first experience, to feel the contrast of cold water against my warm skin. Lily pads spread out before me like floating islands, green on top and deep crimson underneath, attached to delicate stems the same shade of crimson, rooted in the muddy bottom. The stems and undersides of the pads were coated with a clear, slippery gel. I parted them like a curtain and slowly immersed myself in cool, silken water, swimming languidly out to meet Tom at the center of the pond. I think of water as a basic medium for healing and could feel myself coming back to life.

We were starving after our swim. The house was bereft of food, so we showered, dressed, and drove to a bakery for hot coffee and fresh croissants. Our next stop was a market in the center of town to get groceries. There was something grounding about eating breakfast and buying food. On the ride back, I turned to Tom and said, "I want to draw." It was such a simple statement.

Tom asked, "What do you have in mind?"

"I don't know. It's a feeling, like a part of me is coming back online. I know I said I wasn't bringing any art supplies, but I did pack a couple sticks of vine charcoal and a drawing pad just in case . . ."

"I had a thought. Want to hear it?"

"Yeah."

"How about self-portraits? What about starting with you as your subject, where you are now?"

I rolled that possibility over in my mind, beginning to feel the wheels turning: *My face . . . beneath all of the masks.* I said to Tom, "I think you're right."

Tom parked the car and we carried our groceries up the ramp and into the kitchen. My mind was humming. *Wasn't there a mirror in the bedroom? I'll need a mirror . . . and an easel. Where am I going to get an easel? And a chair. There's got to be something in one of the guest rooms that will work.* I had forgotten what it felt like to be high on a creative idea.

Tom said, "I'll put this stuff away. You need to get to work."

In an hour, I had everything set up. A full-length mirror leaned against one of the bedroom walls. A window that opened onto Higgins Pond had good natural light. In a storage area under the house, I found the discarded frame of an old wooden director's chair that I turned into an easel. I placed my drawing pad on the easel and flipped a wastebasket upside down to hold the sticks of charcoal. My heart was pounding. Was it exhilaration or fear? Closing my eyes, I told myself, *Slow down, savor this moment. You have all the time in the world.* The words were soothing. My body relaxed. My breathing slowed to match the cadence of the voice in my mind. I opened my eyes to look at the face in the mirror.

I SAW AN AGING WOMAN WITH UNRULY hair that caught the light at crown and temples. Brown curls around her face were tangled up in a nest of white hair. Her pale eyelashes would be invisible without the mascara and eyeliner she used every morning to frame her green eyes, the one part of her face that hadn't changed over the years. Smile lines were etched like parentheses at the corners of her mouth, and fine wrinkles around her eyes fanned out like wings. Two worry lines marked the boundary between her eyebrows. As I looked at her without judgment, the journey of my life was imprinted on her face like a pictograph. I felt compelled to tell her story, the story that was mine.

Drawing with soft vine charcoal is like painting. A stroke of my finger, moving fluidly across the marks on paper, is like a sable brush softening a line, creating shadows, defining shapes. I started with the eyes, deep-set, and smudged shadows beneath them. Quick strokes sketched in nose and mouth, the angle of cheekbone and jaw, neck, and shoulders. The sharpened end of a charcoal stick delicately laid down lines and wrinkles, and suggested a swath of white hair.

When I stepped back from this first self-portrait, I saw my history writ deeper than words. Like a Maori face tattoo signifying identity and origins, my wrinkles told the story of who I was and who I was becoming, a beautiful old woman. Although I didn't choose all of it, I'd lived all of it. My journey was worthy of self-respect. It was time for me to face the truth of this.

I was on fire to make art, so the next day I claimed the guest bedroom for my studio and moved everything out but the bed. A built-in corner desk with bookshelves on either side became my worktable and storage space. I left the easel in our bedroom next to the mirror, just in case I needed it. I already had the self-portrait as reference material. My drawing pad lay next to it on the desk, open to an empty white page, along with a flat carpenter's pencil I found in one of the kitchen drawers.

Staring into the eyes of my drawing, a nightmare from the night before flashed into my mind. All I could remember was waking up terrified, and the words *You will have to confront your demons.* My first thought was *Fuck the demons!* Then I realized with a jolt that my muse had returned. I could feel her presence, intense and confrontative. No longer the playmate of my childhood, nor my inspiration as an emerging artist, she challenged me. *Did you actually think that acknowledging getting old was the end of it? That was only the beginning. You've just caught up with yourself.* An image of my second self-portrait began to emerge. It was the face of death.

On the right side I replicated my first self-portrait, but much older, with a closed eye, a more pronounced cheekbone, and thin lips. My hair had receded, leaving nothing but a smooth dome of skull. My face was peaceful. Death was on the left side. Soft tissue had fallen away, revealing the skull: teeth and bone, hollow caverns of the nasal cavity and eye socket. When I stepped back to look at what I had drawn, I saw an eye looking out at me from the shadow where my eye had been, as if saying, *I know you.*

Of course you do.

We met mid-November 1989. I had just been diagnosed with kidney cancer. Surgery was the only effective treatment. A radical nephrectomy was scheduled the day before Thanksgiving to remove my left kidney.

For nearly thirty years that day has been our anniversary.
For nearly thirty years you have been my companion.

The first year after surgery was marked by my fear of dying and the intensity of being alive. I was in a new relationship and in love with life. Everything was bittersweet. I am not sentimental about holidays, but at Christmas simply buying a tree, tying it to the top of the car, and the smell of pine in the crisp night air brought tears to my eyes. I wanted to gather together all the people I loved and hold them close to my heart. I did not want to let them go. As we celebrated each holiday, I wondered if it would be my last. I could feel, rather than hear, a metronome marking time. I knew it could stop at any moment.

The almost-unendurable part was the checkups, every three months the first year, to see if the cancer had metastasized. There were two tests: a urinalysis and a chest X-ray. I'd go to the lab for the urinalysis, sit in a nondescript waiting room, and listen for my name to be called. I would be given a small plastic cup with a lid and directed to the restroom. I am not Catholic, but it felt like going to confession, as if I had done something wrong. Not a sin exactly, but something like it. *Cancer* is such a terrifying word, a forbidden word, that most people are uncomfortable even talking about. So I'd pee in the cup, place it carefully on a small shelf above the toilet so it wouldn't spill, and walk back down the hall. I felt like a supplicant praying for absolution. At the end of eight years, with the results of every test coming up negative, I was pronounced cured.

The core teaching in *The Tibetan Book of Living and Dying* is to practice dying. I learned, in those eight years, when the reality of death was so close, that death is not the opposite of life. It is a part of life. And life is precious beyond measure. Why had this memory surfaced so powerfully for me in Cape Cod? I turned seventy-two the month Tom and I were there. I was getting old. I began to know in the depths of my being that the beat of the metronome would stop for me—in two decades? In one? I didn't want to miss any of it. Even the terrifying parts.

The following morning, a purging came without warning, like a waking nightmare. Shit erupted softly, warm, filling my underwear and oozing down my pantleg. Thank God I was at home. I excused myself from the breakfast table and walked to the bathroom, closing the door behind me. The release was uncontrollable. I stripped off my clothes and stepped into the shower. Hot water and shit ran down the drain until the water ran clear. I washed myself, rinsed my soiled clothing, and cleaned the bathroom floor. When I told Tom why I had left the table so abruptly he was sympathetic, but I felt troubled throughout the day, and off-balance. Since the Butte Fire, this was the second time a purging had happened. After trauma, it's not only the mind that needs to release fear and helplessness for healing to occur; the body does as well. Still, repeating this disconcerting and humiliating experience left me feeling apprehensive and on guard. I didn't know when it would happen again.

The next morning after our swim, my head was clearer, and my body felt cleansed by the cold water. A poem by Wendell Berry came to mind:

> *To know the dark, go dark. Go without sight,*
> *and find that the dark, too, blooms and sings,*
> *and is traveled by dark feet and dark wings.*

Pondering the meaning of the poem, I wandered outside to enjoy the warmth of a pale autumn sun when I saw a manhole cover stamped with the word *SEWER*. Running into the house like a madwoman, I found a stick of charcoal and my drawing pad and ran back out to do a rubbing, several actually. Each imprint was unique. I took them into the living room and spread them across the floor. We had built a fire in the fireplace the night before. What remained was ash and burnt pieces of wood. I had all the materials I needed to draw my third self-portrait.

I sat on the brick hearth, the tablet in front of me, with one of the rubbings on top. I smeared a handful of ash over the word *SEWER* and attacked one side of the paper with ragged hash marks using pieces of burnt wood. Just above the word, I drew two frightened eyes in a face partially obscured by the letters S-E-W-E-R. I felt exhilarated and unrestrained as I rubbed my bare feet with charcoal and stomped on the paper, first the left foot and then the right. "To know the dark, go dark. Go without sight." I did that, not knowing where I was going, trusting the process. It felt I had taken the waste from my burned-up studio and made art out of it. I had transformed the shit!

Depression is a clinical word. The medical model does not allow for sacred suffering, preferring instead to diagnose depression as a mental illness and treat it with medication. I was not mentally ill. I was on a journey, a dark night of the soul. The first three self-portraits had revealed my deepest fears. I had to go into the unknown to meet myself growing old. I could not be fully alive without making space in my mind for the reality of my death. Only then could the darkness bloom and sing for me.

I began to hunger for color, as if color was food for my eyes. I could almost taste it. We found an art store in nearby Provincetown. When I opened the door, it was like opening my Christmas present. Everything I wanted was inside. Colored pencils, tubes of acrylic paint in myriad colors, whole rows of brushes. Tablets of art paper stacked on shelves were spread out before me like treasure. I was overwhelmed by my desire for color. Tom said, "Your birthday's coming up. Choose whatever you want. It's my present."

I hadn't purchased art materials since my studio burned down. My heart had not been in it. So much was irreplaceable.

I had lost everything and didn't know where to start until that moment. I began filling a shopping basket with acrylic colors in my palette: cadmium yellow and red, quinacridone burnt orange, cerulean blue and ultramarine violet, Hooker's green, Payne's gray, and the iridescent colors. Just saying their names in my mind was like remembering a forgotten language. I stroked brushes to find just the right ones and felt the texture of paper before settling on an eighteen-inch-by-thirty-six-inch tablet of Arches watercolor paper. While checking out, I spied a tin of forty-eight Prismacolor pencils. It was a huge extravagance, but I added them to my purchases as if they were a box of Godiva chocolates. The drive home felt expansive. I now had an abundance of supplies for my studio and for my soul to do creative work.

THE NEXT DAY, HIGGINS POND BECKONED me just as the sun was rising. The sky was deep blue, with brushstrokes of orange and gold on the horizon. Tom was still asleep. I didn't want to wake him, so I wrapped myself in a towel for warmth against the early morning chill and tiptoed out of our bedroom. The water was so cold I had to swim fast to keep warm. Then a kind of hypothermia set in. I relaxed and let my body sink until it was vertical, with my head above water, arms on the surface, and hands paddling gently to keep me afloat. I allowed myself to be cradled by the water. It was a liminal moment, suspended between earth and sky.

After a hot shower and warm breakfast, I began the fourth self-portrait, using translucent washes of color to capture the morning's experience: the timeless sense of floating with my head above water, my body below, and feeling the surface of the pond, as well as its depths. Lily pads surrounded me, trailing their stems like the tentacles of jellyfish. I felt at one with the sky, with the water, and with myself.

Our month on the cape was almost over. Tom had completed the final draft of *The Restless Hungarian* in this house, built by his father the year he was born. Coming home to complete his memoir was also an emotional journey for him, and a time for healing. In the final paragraph of his book, Tom wrote, "I believe there is a point, a purpose, in descending into the depths of the past and befriending the sorrowful souls who still dwell in our hearts . . . hoping not only to make them completely real in my heart, but perhaps reaching through the veil of time and space, to let them know that they are truly seen, honored, and loved. I say to them, 'Look, dear family. I am well. I am alive. And I embrace you.'"

It was the end of September. Days were getting shorter and colder, and rain came more frequently. Before we left, I had to swim one last time and do one more self-portrait. I drew myself sitting cross-legged on a cushion, naked, the way I had felt on the flight to Cape Cod, and draped strands of dark-red water lilies around my breasts and belly. My eyes were closed as if still in that liquid dream space. I understood how important it had been to come naked and vulnerable, stripped of my defenses so I could be healed. I, too, felt well and alive.

Chapter 35

WE CAME HOME A MONTH BEFORE the 2016 presidential election. National and state polls had predicted that Hillary Clinton would win, but the results on election night rolled in like a mega thunderstorm that hit under the radar. Clinton had won the popular vote, but Donald Trump won the electoral college. No one who had voted for Clinton imagined we would be watching her concession speech the next morning.

As increasingly disturbing information about Trump's presidency erupted daily in the news, I forced myself to see reality. Trump had the power to manifest his agenda with a Republican majority in the House and the Senate. I learned to titrate my morning dose of the *New York Times* so I wouldn't feel despair for the rest of the day. I tried watching *Saturday Night Live* for comic relief, but the black humor was too close to reality and left me feeling more like sobbing than laughing.

Václav Havel, while imprisoned for speaking out against political oppression in Czechoslovakia, defined hope as follows:

> A state of mind, not a state of the world. It is an orientation of the spirit, an orientation of the heart. . . . Hope, in

this deep and powerful sense is . . . an ability to work for something because it is good, not just because it stands a chance to succeed.

I was devastated by what seemed like the dismantling of everything I believed in. Where could I even begin to work for what was good?

On January 21, 2017, the day after Trump's inauguration, people in cities all over the world gathered for the Women's March, a peaceful protest against Trump's commitment to weaken environmental protection and his egregious disrespect for basic human rights. It was the largest single-day protest in US history. Tom and I joined twenty thousand people in Sacramento. It felt like a massive family reunion. We were angry. We were grieving and afraid, but we were also in community, claiming the right to speak our truth out loud to power. The protest signs said it succinctly:

No Racism, No Sexism, No Xenophobia, No Ableism,
No Homophobia, NO TRUMP!
Deny Trump, Not Climate
D-I-G-N-I-T-Y
Grab Back
My Anger Is Justified
I Choose to Love
We Can Do It

We came together for something good, not knowing if it stood a chance of changing the reality of the next four years. I went home feeling inspired.

THE FOLLOWING WEEK, MY PSYCHOLOGIST shared the chorus from a Leonard Cohen song, "Anthem":

Ring the bells that still can ring
Forget your perfect offering
There is a crack, a crack in everything
That's how the light gets in.

There was something compelling about the words "That's how the light gets in," in juxtaposition with Wendell Berry's poem, "To Know the Dark."

I felt creative tension urging me back to work. Since the Butte Fire, except for Cape Cod and the self-portraits, I had been unable to make art, even though I had a studio in our home. It felt unfamiliar. Nothing had my scent, the smell of my materials, or the mess of my projects, like an artist's scat marking the territory. But what had opened up for me in Cape Cod was real. Whenever I've been hurt, and scared, and stuck, I've made art, not knowing where it would take me. As a country, it felt as if we were at the beginning of our own Dark Ages. To know how to live in that darkness, I needed to go into the dark. I started with a four-by-eight-foot composition board and painted it black. Leaning against a wall in my studio, it looked like an enormous headstone.

The next morning, I woke up abruptly. Etched in my mind was a line drawing of an elongated diamond with rounded sides, white against a black background. Where had I seen it? Then I remembered a prehistoric image of the divine feminine, the vagina. I laughed softly. It was the sacred crack that opens to let light in during birth.

Forget breakfast! I threw on sweats, turned on the light in my studio, and rummaged around looking for a stick of white chalk. I marked the exact center of my board and drew the ancient symbol. Release poured through my body. Trusting the process, I waited for what would come next.

Memories of the Women's March in Sacramento began to fill my mind, the communal joy of marching together in solidarity for what was good, pictures of ten thousand people in

Washington, DC, with the Capitol dome in the background, and the sea of bright-pink pussy hats protesting Trump's misogyny. They'd gone viral almost overnight, as if the entire female population on the planet had come out of the closet saying, "We're female, we're proud of it, and we're pissed off."

The symbol of the sacred feminine was a starting point. I was inspired by Judy Chicago's 1979 installation, *The Dinner Party*, and wanted to take more risks. In a darkened room, she had arranged three tables in a triangle covered in fine linen, set for thirty-nine women, historical and mythical, who had changed the world. For every place setting, Chicago created a porcelain dinner plate of the vagina, exquisitely sculpted in bas-relief to honor each guest. Judy Chicago's celebration of female identity was unflinching, her message as important four decades ago as it was now.

The Joy of Sex hadn't been published until I was in my late twenties. I'd gone through a divorce and was in my second marriage with three kids. I didn't hear the word *clitoris* spoken until I was in my thirties. Since before I could remember, it had been my secret. Although I learned the word *masturbation* when I was a teenager in the early 1960s, it still carried a heavy load of guilt. But *clitoris* sounded light, almost musical. It made me happy to know the part of me that first gave comfort, and then pleasure, had a name. I didn't just want to say it; I wanted to paint it "out loud."

I drew the folds of the labia and hooded clitoris in realistic detail. The colors seemed to choose themselves in rich shades of red, gold, and blue acrylic paint, with the sacred crack iridescent white. But something was missing. I stood back, impatient for inspiration, when I saw flames from the Butte Fire at the base of the image and dark wings hovering above it. The dark and the light were in dialogue. As I completed the painting, it came to life with a vividness and authenticity all its own.

In naming my painting *The Sacred Crack*, I felt a sense of sisterhood with Eve Ensler, author of *The Vagina Monologues*, and with women all over the world who had shared their stories to "honor female sexuality in all its complexity, and call for a world where all women are safe, equal, free, and alive in their bodies." I thought of my painting as part of the ongoing conversation.

A few weeks after I finished *The Sacred Crack*, I showed it to a close friend who is also an artist. He looked at it thoughtfully, then said that the figure looked a lot like the Virgin of Guadalupe. My immediate reaction was, "You're kidding, right? A virgin?" I had painted an image of fertility, an ancient symbol of female sexuality. I couldn't imagine it in any way representing a virgin.

He said, "Yeah, take a closer look . . . the blue hooded cape, the red gown, the light . . ."

Then I remembered the riotous celebration of the Virgin of Guadalupe on the day Tom and I arrived in Sucre, and the voluptuous young women who danced so provocatively before the virgin and for the eyes of young men. The dissonance between an anatomically correct painting of a vagina and the fully clothed Catholic icon of a virgin was so unexpected that I had to Google her story. It goes like this:

A brown-skinned virgin appeared to an indigenous man in 1531, ten years after the Spanish conquest of Mexico, and asked him to build a little house for her on a hill outside of what is now Mexico City. Her life was dedicated to caring for people in the village with deep compassion and love, and she became the patron saint of Mexico. To this day, the Virgin of Guadalupe is venerated as a champion of oppressed people, whatever society they live in.

I needed to rethink my bias. Given her struggle for justice during a time when indigenous people had been conquered and subjugated, she belonged in the conversation about women's identity, sexuality, and power in the face of patriarchy. I felt blessed by her appearance in my painting.

Chapter 36

THE SACRED CRACK **WAS A FULCRUM,** the still point of balance between the dark and the light. Now I wanted to explore each polarity in depth. I started with Wendell Berry's "dark feet and dark wings," imagining a luminous S-curve sweeping diagonally across the night sky, filled with creatures mythical and real, walking, slithering, and taking flight.

I made charcoal sketches of the mutated snakes, frogs, and flightless birds that I found in the dramatic red and black weaving by Adela, the Jalq'a woman Tom and I had met in Bolivia. I added bizarre creatures from Hieronymus Bosch's medieval triptych, *The Garden of Earthly Delight*, including a dog doing a balancing act with no front legs, a dancing kangaroo with a rat's head, and a demonic-looking hedgehog. Finally, I drew the spiders, beetles, owls, vultures, and bats that lived on our land. I was calling them from the collective unconscious, from different cultures, different places, and different times.

At first, they were frightening beings, but drawing them was an intimate encounter. I could not bring the creatures to life, each one in its individuality, if I objectified them. During our shared experience, they became my familiars. In my second painting, *To Know the Dark*, we had gone on a journey together and I could hear their song.

A year and a half after Trump took office, I started the third painting, *The Light Gets In*. Trump's attacks against the environment, women, minorities, and anyone who challenged him continued unabated. Republicans in Congress were more committed to party loyalty and reelection than the welfare of their constituents. The Supreme Court had a conservative bias for the first time in fifty years.

The Women's March had been the first crack in Trump's White House. Others followed. Four months later *The Guardian* reported, "We are in an extraordinary era of protest. Over the course of the first 15 months of the 45th presidency, more people have joined demonstrations than at any other time in American history."

The final work in my trilogy began as a mixed-media collage of images cut from newspaper photos. The United States Capitol building has a jagged crack splitting it down the center and the Statue of Freedom is about to fall. Spilling out of the crack like a river of light are people marching from Occupy Wall Street, Black Lives Matter, the Women's March, and Never Again. All the movements didn't start with Trump, nor did the fight for justice. Although I live and work in a small rural county where the majority voted for Trump, I felt part of a larger community challenging the values he represented and his abuses of power. It gave me hope.

Two weeks later, I was jogging through the living room in stockinged feet, looking for my boots to go on a hike with Tom, when I fell hard on our cement floor and fractured my left femur.

My story began here, but this is not the ending.

Chapter 37

WE PULLED INTO OUR DRIVEWAY, leaving everything in the car. As soon as we walked through our front door, I felt the familiar enveloping space inside our straw-bale house and the smell of it, like dry, clean earth. Tom and I walked from room to room as if greeting some part of ourselves we had left behind when we'd left just two months earlier for a sabbatical in the south of France. It was good to be home. Although sessions with clients would start in two days, we had plenty of time to ease into ordinary life: shopping at Save Mart to replenish the pantry, having dinner at our favorite Italian restaurant, reconnecting with family and friends.

I also had an appointment coming up for something out of the ordinary: a guided journey using psilocybin. I wanted to honor my seventy-fifth year with a rite of passage into the last stage of life, to go into the underworld of my psyche while I had courage enough and time.

On a Thursday evening, three weeks since we'd been back, Tom drove us into the mountains above San Francisco Bay to a secluded retreat surrounded by towering redwoods and incense cedars. When our car pulled into the driveway, my guide, a slender woman with silver streaks in her hair, came out to greet us.

"Hello. It's good you're here before dark. How was your drive?" I felt the warmth of her smile and gentle voice, softened by a French accent. She led us down a gravel path to a small cottage a short distance from her home where I would stay for the next twenty-four hours. I was the only guest that weekend, but Tom could be with me overnight until my journey began at 8:30 the next morning.

We snuggled under quilts on a futon in the center of the room. Tom wrapped his arms around me as I nestled into his body, reminiscing about the mushroom trip I had taken twenty years earlier. It was indescribably beautiful, but also dark and terrifying. Because I had no support in navigating that experience, this time I chose my guide carefully. She had worked for decades with indigenous medicine rituals for healing, and I trusted her.

The next morning Tom held me close and kissed me goodbye as if I were going away for a long time. I took a shower, dressed in loose, comfortable clothes, and sat on a bench near the cottage in the early morning sunlight, enfolded in one of the quilts. I sipped from a cup of water while waiting for my guide, my mind quiet, grateful for these few minutes of solitude.

The ritual began with a prayer of gratitude for the sacred medicine. My guide offered five delicate mushrooms on a small wooden tray with a tiny saucer of honey. I dipped each one in the honey and chewed slowly, tasting sweetness mixed with the dry texture of the mushrooms. I was given a dark mask to cover my eyes, and I lay back on a futon in the center of the room against soft pillows. The room felt comforting. Soothing music played in the background. I waited.

An intense sensation enveloped my body in a hot cocoon. Waves of heat and cold followed. I shivered, then sweated. Tendrils of energy moved through me. Whether my eyes were open or closed behind the mask, I was mesmerized by a bottomless labyrinth of dazzling light so compelling I could not look away. It seemed to go on forever, vibrating with all the colors of the spectrum. Then a grid made from black bands of iron covered the labyrinth. Fluorescent colors flashed in the cracks. My heart pounded. My belly heaved with fear. One word echoed in my mind like a mantra: *allow . . . allow . . . allow*. The ordeal had begun.

The scene shifted; images came in fragments. They were crumbs left on a trail of memory. I fell into a dark hole, alone and afraid, with no place to go, no safe place. I began to retch. My guide came with her soft voice and soft hands. She held my head as I vomited into a bowl, stroking my hair and murmuring, "I am here."

I remembered being alone in the middle of the night, bent over the toilet, throwing up quietly so I wouldn't disturb my parents. I began to sob, "I was always alone . . . I feel scared . . . I'm scared of waking up the sleeping giant," and then I was riding another wave of the journey.

I smelled my father's cigarette smoke, the bourbon on his breath, what it felt like when he held me on his lap. These memories were buried so deeply that only my body could tell the story. My mind was on fire with an unspeakable sadness I had carried for as long as I can remember. *Why do I sleep facing the door? Why do I feel melancholy when dusk comes? Why do I sometimes wake up with sadness that feels as if flows in my veins?*

Then I felt my father's betrayal. I felt my mother's rage toward him and toward me, and her competitiveness. She had a way of disappearing me. These thoughts flashed in my mind, each a piece of the puzzle I had to connect so that I could be whole. She was also betrayed. Like me, she survived by not knowing.

Thoughts cascaded like an avalanche in my mind. They were not logical or cohesive, but they felt true in my gut. I followed the crumbs, picking each one up, "tasting" it. Knowing. There were generations in my family of men who had sexually abused daughters, stepdaughters, granddaughters, nieces, men who betrayed their wives. There were generations of women disempowered, shackled by a code of silence and shame. I felt it in every cell of my body. I screamed in rage. My heart broke open. I screamed and screamed—and then there was stillness. I waited for the next surge.

It was warm and liquid. Soothing. Calm. It filled my being. I thought about my children, Jim and Lisa and Christa. They were grown now with children and grandchildren of their own. They came from me and I held them, one at a time, in the warmth. I held my Tom and felt the blessing of our love. I felt the fragments of my life knitting together.

Tom came at the appointed time to pick me up, but I had a horrendous headache and couldn't eat or drink anything, so we stayed overnight in the cabin. After a ragged sleep, we drove home early the next morning. I napped on and off, but by afternoon I was too weak and dizzy to get out of bed. Thinking that my symptoms were a physical reaction to an intensely emotional experience, I was surprised that they had lasted so long after the journey. Tom decided to call 911, even though that was the last thing I wanted. I was afraid of being judged by a young EMT thinking that I was just an old woman tripping on 'shrooms, who got in over her head.

Thirty minutes later, a man and a woman in their midtwenties came into our bedroom, where I lay curled up on the bed. The woman asked, "What happened?" Her question hung in the air. I felt exposed and vulnerable. The journey was mine. It was private. I had shared it with no one but Tom.

"My wife had psilocybin mushrooms twenty-four hours ago," Tom reported. "We think she got dehydrated. She's been throwing up and can't keep anything down, not even water."

I glanced up at her. She had a look of bemused respect

in her eyes and said, "Yeah. The day after you can feel like shit." Her partner took my vitals while she gathered more information. They decided I didn't need to be transported by ambulance to the ER. My husband could take me. As they gathered up their stuff, the man turned to me and said, "A friend of mine told me that smoking weed can help."

Relief flooded over me and I laughed.

Five hours and two intravenous liters of saline later, we drove home from the ER, watched a movie halfway through, and then I slept for ten hours.

ON SUNDAY MORNING, I WOKE UP feeling like the survivor of a private disaster. Munching a few crackers between sips of water, I ventured outside and heard the screech of a hawk in the distance. The day felt new.

My journey, I now understood, was a portal into the next phase of life. I was becoming an old woman, an elder. I had wanted a transformative, "spiritual," experience. What I got was a stark confrontation with the darkness and light, the terror and magnificence of being alive, and the realization that my childhood memories of trauma, and the abuse my family had kept secret for generations, were real. It was what I needed to heal. There were times when my mind became quiet, but the silence was not empty. It was a kind of presence, a soft thrumming. I felt a sense of peace.

A week later, on March 17, 2020, I had to cancel all of my therapy groups and arrange for phone sessions with individual clients. We began sheltering in place. COVID-19 had struck.

For the rest of the spring and into the summer, it felt as if the future had gone missing. I did routine things like scheduling phone sessions with clients, checking out what was in the fridge for dinner, and making to-do lists, but I couldn't seem to think beyond trying, each day, to adapt to the pandemic. I made masks for Tom and myself from handkerchiefs I found in one of our drawers. I made alcohol hand sanitizer with aloe gel. We kept in touch with family and friends via email, texting, and FaceTime. YouTube videos of people in cities around the globe making music from balconies, windows, and rooftops gave me momentary hope. I read the *New York Times* every morning to track the spread of the virus. But I didn't have a word for what it felt like living in relative safety on twenty acres with no mortgage and a job I could do from home when so many people were suffering.

There was too much happening, one crisis after another with no relief: George Floyd's murder, wildfires burning all summer from California to the Canadian border, and the worsening pandemic. I felt helpless and afraid of what would happen next, afraid of COVID, of Trump being reelected, of running out of time to save the planet. I wanted to live before I died—and I didn't want to live in lockdown.

Then, in late September, I woke up before the alarm and walked outside. The temperature gauge read ninety-eight degrees. A gust of wind blew a pile of dry oak leaves across the brick patio, sounding like a million tiny castanets playing a raspy tune. I looked out over our land, the color of buckskin. The sky was a clear blue, free of smoke for the first time in a month. I could breathe easily. In that moment, I realized I was just where I belonged, in this place, at this time. I went back into the house feeling at peace. I didn't check my newsfeed.

AN UNEXPECTED GIFT OF SHELTERING in place was learning to slow down, pay attention to what might otherwise seem ordinary, and breathe. For about three weeks, an elegant lizard we named Lenny had been hanging out on my window-sill. He'd come every day, usually around noon, from some mysterious place in my writing studio and roam up and down the screen in search of insects. I'd give him water in a jar lid and talk to him in a quiet voice. He never darted away. Once, I was sitting at my worktable talking on the phone when I spied Lenny only inches away from me, exploring my open laptop. Surprised, I shifted in my chair and caught his attention. He looked at me as if to say, *What?* and then continued to make his way across the keyboard. He felt like my cross-species buddy, and I looked forward to his visits. Then one day he didn't come.

"Lenny, where are you?" I asked in a soft voice. I looked in the shady places on the window casement where he hid from the heat at midday and searched in every corner of the studio. No luck.

The next day, I noticed a large Styrofoam lid lying on the floor in the laundry room and picked it up. There was Lenny, sitting on a strip of cardboard packaging, resting peacefully in the shadow of the lid. I greeted him and left a jar lid of water nearby. Two days later he was still there. I was worried that he might be starving—or dying. Tears came to my eyes. In this time of isolation, he'd become my steady companion. I carefully lifted the piece of cardboard up with Lenny on top and placed it on the window ledge in my studio. He didn't budge. In the morning, Lenny was still there. Without moving his body, he turned his head and looked at me with one beady eye. I whispered, "You need food. I'm going to find some."

Out in our garden, I turned over rocks and scanned the dry earth for insects. After fifteen minutes in the hot sun, I only found two tiny pill bugs, but I brought them to Lenny anyway. One of them got stuck in some adhesive on the cardboard and wiggled around helplessly. Lenny saw it but didn't respond. I touched the spot and could barely lift my finger off. Then I realized, *Oh my God, he can't move.* I looked closer. The right edge of his body and his right hind foot were stuck to the cardboard. He'd gone three days without food or water.

I located a bottle of nail polish remover under the bathroom sink to see if I could use it as a solvent to set him free. It didn't work. Then I found a sharp X-ACTO knife. I told Lenny in a calm voice what I was going to do, like the dentist does before he puts sharp things in your mouth, and I cut into the cardboard to free his belly. He tried frantically to get away, but five delicate toes were still stuck. I worked carefully, afraid that if I slipped I would amputate one. With the last toe, Lenny catapulted himself off the ledge. Debris was still attached to his foot, but he was alive.

There is a way that seemingly random events can come together, opening doors to understanding. The next day Lenny was back in the studio, climbing up the window screen to hunt for insects, but I continued to feel shaken by the torrent of emotions that had been unleashed in me as I was trying to free him. Why did it take so long for me to see that he was stuck? Then I realized parallels with the COVID pandemic: my sense of being stuck in time and place, the loss of freedom, being afraid of hurting someone unintentionally, and trying to figure out how to live each day when nothing seemed normal. How can any of us feel the enormity of the pandemic, the threat it represents on a personal, national, and global level? It's impossible. So, my pervasive sense of fear and helplessness stayed stuck somewhere inside me until an intimate experience with a wild creature I had come to love loosened it a little bit.

As Lenny's foot healed, he became more active in his forays across the window screen, and our life resumed its normal routine. But one day he didn't show up. I scoured the house looking for him, but there was no sign of Lenny anywhere. After a week, I knew he wasn't coming home. I thought of the cliché "If you love someone, set them free." He had set himself free, probably through a door inadvertently left open to the world outside. Whenever a lizard darted across the patio or up a wall, I'd look to see if it was Lenny, but I never saw him again.

THE BUILDUP TO ELECTION DAY was almost unbearable. Like my grandmother, I'm a "free-thinker," a registered Democrat, and I've never missed voting in any election. But I was scared—no, terrified—about the outcome of this one. No president in my lifetime had been as destructive and divisive as Trump, nor as vicious in pitting one group of Americans against another. We needed leadership that could unify us. Tom and I drove our mail-in ballots to the drop box at the Angels Camp Save Mart.

A middle-aged woman wearing a mask, rubber gloves, and a baseball cap with the store logo was outside disinfecting grocery carts. Seeing the envelopes in our hands, she said, "The place you're looking for is just inside the entrance on the left."

We found ourselves standing in front of a yellow, white, and blue "Official Ballot Drop Box" emblazoned with a large "I Voted" sticker. Tom dropped his envelope in first, but I hesitated. It was such a strange polling place. Bargain fruits and vegetables were arranged on tables just across the aisle. Shoppers passed by on their way to the exit pushing carts laden with groceries. Everywhere was movement and noise. I just wanted to get it over with and get out of the store, but as I reached out to put my envelope in the slot, everything slowed down. I realized the importance of my individual act. All across the country, in big cities and small, in rural communities like ours, people were voting. I released my envelope to join all the others. Two months later, watching the inauguration of Joseph Biden and Kamala Harris, I felt hope for the first time in four years.

Epilogue

I HAVE MARKED MY ADULT LIFE in ten-year lengths of time, with significant change beginning at the midpoint. This book spans the decade from age sixty-five to seventy-five, the most turbulent and transformative period of my life.

As with any initiation, preparation begins before the journey. When I turned sixty, I did not want to lament aging. I wanted no "over the hill" parties that turned this rite of passage into a sad comedy. I decided to have a Croning Ritual, to honor becoming an old woman, and invited ten friends to a brunch at my house. Two women, who were older than me, offered to guide the ritual.

On the morning of my birthday, the kitchen smelled of cinnamon, bread fresh out of the oven, and hot coffee. After brunch we sat in a circle, quiet and expectant. All eyes turned toward me, and my face flushed as Marylu placed a crown of ribbons and flowers on my head. Gay invited each woman to share what I meant to her and told me not to speak until the sharing was complete. I looked into my friends' eyes as they told their stories. I felt respected and loved as a friend and as an elder.

"Coming of age" usually means transitioning from adolescence into adulthood. In our culture, it is mythologized in television series, young adult books, memoirs, and films. But as a woman coming of age as an elder, where are the stories that guide initiation into the last stage of life? Who are the wise ones to welcome us home after an ordeal, to acknowledge that we are valuable to the community, and to celebrate the gifts we bring?

My daughter Lisa asked me recently why I have taken so many risks. I didn't have a ready answer for her. But now, I think I needed to look death in the face, the inevitability of it, and to savor my precious years of getting old, rather than fear them. I realize that this last decade has been an initiation, with separation, ordeal, and homecomings, some intentional and some that came unbidden: trekking the Himalayas, building environmental sculptures for Burning Man, meeting the love of my life, making a home with him after losing everything in a devastating forest fire, and living through a global pandemic in a time of political crisis.

One thing I know is true. The whole of life is here for us in each moment if we stop and savor it. Rilke wrote a hundred years ago, "And the point is, to live everything. *Live* the questions now. Perhaps then, someday far in the future, you will gradually, without even noticing it, live your way into the answer." Having already lived far into the future, I have learned that some questions have no answers . . . and those are the most precious ones.

Acknowledgments

THE TITLE OF MY BOOK WAS MY husband Tom's inspiration. He was by my side every step of the journey, and our love story is at the heart of my memoir.

I raised my children, Jim, Lisa, and Christa, to be exactly who they are, to take risks, and to explore possibilities. In my elderhood they extend to me the same freedom, to live my life and tell my story in my way.

My friends are chosen family who encouraged me from the beginning: Efren, Cheryl, Dee, Catherine, Black Eagle, and MB (my faithful reader through the whole process), CeeCee and Kathy and the Brunch Bunch, our Elder's Group (John and Rhoda, Jane and Bert), Seth and Carolynn, and Diana (writing buddy and fellow workshop participant).

I cannot forget my clients who enthusiastically supported my taking a two-month sabbatical in the south of France to complete the first draft of *Burning Woman* and continued to check in to see how it was going.

Every therapist needs good counsel. My psychologist, Frank, helped me through the dark times and celebrated the successes with me.

Last, but certainly not least, the dedicated people at She Writes Press. Special thanks to my mentor and coach, Publisher Brooke Warner, and to Editorial Project Manager Shannon Green. The cover design is the art direction of Julie Metz.

Copy editor Victoria Elliott crafted the final manuscript while being beautifully attuned to my writer's voice. Proofreader Barrett Brisk's thoughtful attention to detail completed the editing process.

My guide and publicist, Sylvia Margolin Paull, helped me navigate the treacherous waters of social media, believed in my memoir in its nascent stage, and generously opened doors to give *Burning Woman* a wider audience.

Excerpt from lyrics of "Swimming to the Other Side" reprinted with permission. Copyright 1990 Pat Humphries, Moving Forward Music, BMI. emmasrevolution@me.com.

About the Author

SHARON STRONG is a practicing psychologist and artist, mask-maker, and creator of towering sculptures for Burning Man as well as gallery exhibits in Northern California. She is the illustrator of two books—*Serious Fun: Ingenious Improvisations on Money, Food, Waste, Water & Home*, by Carolyn North, and *Two Lines 13: Masks*, edited by Zack Rogow—and in 2005 she self-published *Soul Unmasked: A Personal Journey into the Ancient Ritual of the Mask*. She lives in Angels Camp, California, on twenty acres in a straw-bale house with her husband, filmmaker Tom Weidlinger, whom she met at age seventy. Their story inspired her to write *Burning Woman*.

Author photo © Tom Weidlinger

SELECTED TITLES FROM SHE WRITES PRESS

She Writes Press is an independent publishing
company founded to serve women writers everywhere.
Visit us at www.shewritespress.com.

The Shelf Life of Ashes: A Memoir by Hollis Giammatteo. $16.95,
978-1-63152-047-1. Confronted by an importuning mother 3,000
miles away who thinks her end is nigh—and feeling ambushed
by her impending middle age—Giammatteo determines to find
The Map of Aging Well, a decision that leads her on an often-
comic journey.

Operatic Divas and Naked Irishmen: An Innkeeper's Tale by
Nancy R. Hinchliff. $16.95, 978-1-63152-194-2. At sixty four,
divorced, retired, and with no prior business experience and little
start-up money, Nancy Hinchliff impulsively moves to a new city
where she knows only one person, buys a 125-year-old historic
mansion, and turns it into a bed and breakfast.

*Flip-Flops After Fifty: And Other Thoughts on Aging I Remembered
to Write Down* by Cindy Eastman. $16.95, 978-1-938314-68-1. A
collection of frank and funny essays about turning fifty—and all
the emotional ups and downs that come with it.

*Renewable: One Woman's Search for Simplicity, Faithfulness,
and Hope* by Eileen Flanagan. $16.95, 978-1-63152-968-9. At age
forty-nine, Eileen Flanagan had an aching feeling that she wasn't
living up to her youthful ideals or potential, so she started trying
to change the world—and in doing so, she found the courage to
change her life.

Seeing Red: A Woman's Quest for Truth, Power, and the Sacred
by Lone Morch. $16.95, 978-1-938314-12-4. One woman's journey
over inner and outer mountains—a quest that takes her to the holy
Mt. Kailas in Tibet, through a seven-year marriage, and into the
arms of the fierce goddess Kali, where she discovers her powerful,
feminine self.